T0001654

2ND EDITION

Birds *of* Oklahoma

Field Guide

Stan Tekiela

PUBLICATIONS
Adventure
an imprint of AdventureKEEN

Edited by Sandy Livoti and Andrew Mollenkof

Cover, book design, and illustrations by Jonathan Norberg

Range maps produced by Anthony Hertzel

Cover photo: Scissor-tailed Flycatcher by Stan Tekiela

All photos by Stan Tekiela except p. 238 (breeding) by **Agami Photo Agency/Shutterstock.com**; pp. 48 (non-breeding male), 114 (non-breeding male), 284 (juvenile) by **Rick & Nora Bowers**; p. 232 (displaying) by **cliff collings/Shutterstock.com**; pp. 74 (female), 124 (female) by **Brian E Kushner/Shutterstock.com**; p. 162 by **Paul Reeves Photography/Shutterstock.com**; pp. 42 (juvenile), 148 (both juveniles), 190 (dark morph, intermediate morph, soaring dark morph), 244 (in-flight) by **Brian K. Wheeler**; and pp. 100 (Oregon female), 188 (female), 240 (main), 246 (female), 300 (female) by **Jim Zipp**.

To the best of the publisher's knowledge, all photos were of live birds. Some were photographed in a controlled condition.

10 9 8 7 6 5 4 3 2 1

Birds of Oklahoma Field Guide
First Edition 2002
Second Edition 2024
Copyright © 2002 and 2024 by Stan Tekiela
Published by Adventure Publications
An imprint of AdventureKEEN
310 Garfield Street South
Cambridge, Minnesota 55008
(800) 678-7006
www.adventurepublications.net

Cataloging-in-Publication data is available from the Library of Congress
ISBN 978-1-64755-437-8 (pbk.); ISBN 978-1-64755-438-5 (ebook)

TABLE OF CONTENTS

WHAT'S NEW?

It is hard to believe that it's been more than 20 years since the debut of *Birds of Oklahoma Field Guide*. This critically acclaimed field guide has helped countless people identify and enjoy the birds that we love. Now, in this expanded second edition, *Birds of Oklahoma Field Guide* has many new and exciting changes and a fresh look, while retaining the same familiar, easy-to-use format.

To help you identify even more birds in Oklahoma, I have added 8 new species and more than 150 new color photographs. All of the range maps have been meticulously reviewed, and many updates have been made to reflect the ever-changing movements of the birds.

Everyone's favorite section, "Stan's Notes," has been expanded to include even more natural history information. "Compare" sections have been updated to help ensure that you correctly identify your bird, and additional feeder information has been added to help with bird feeding. I hope you will enjoy this great new edition as you continue to learn about and appreciate our Oklahoma birds!

WHY WATCH BIRDS IN OKLAHOMA?

Millions of people have discovered bird feeding. It's a simple and enjoyable way to bring the beauty of birds closer to your home. Watching birds at your feeder often leads to a lifetime pursuit of bird identification. The *Birds of Oklahoma Field Guide* is for those who want to identify common birds of Oklahoma.

There are over 900 species of birds found in North America. In Oklahoma alone there have been more than 425 different kinds of birds recorded through the years. These bird sightings were diligently recorded by hundreds of bird watchers and became part of the official state record. From these valuable records, I've chosen 123 of the most common birds of Oklahoma to include in this field guide.

Bird watching, often called birding, is one of the most popular activities in America. Its outstanding appeal in Oklahoma is due, in part, to an unusually rich and abundant birdlife. Why are there so many birds? One reason is open space. Oklahoma is over 69,500 square miles (180,700 sq. km), making it the twentieth largest state. Despite its large size, only about 4 million people call Oklahoma home. On average, that is only 60 people per square mile (22 per sq. km). Most of these people are located in and around only three major cities in eastern Oklahoma.

Open space is not the only reason there is such an abundance of birds. It's also the diversity of habitat. The state can be broken into several distinct habitats, each of which supports a different group of birds.

The western three-quarters of the state is the highest and driest part of Oklahoma. This region is known as the Interior Plains or High Plains. Many open-country birds are found here, such as Horned Larks, Lark Buntings, and Western Kingbirds.

The Coastal Plain is a narrow strip located in eastern Oklahoma. It's wetter, with several rivers creating wide flat bottomlands covered with forest. The oak-hickory forests here are home to birds such as Great Crested Flycatchers and Summer Tanagers.

Between these two regions is the Interior Highlands. The broad, flat-topped hills and rugged ridges and valleys in this area are covered mostly with pine trees. This region is a good place to see Cedar Waxwings and Ruby-throated Hummingbirds.

Water also plays a part in the state's bird populations. Oklahoma has several major rivers, such as the Arkansas and Red Rivers, and many man-made reservoirs such as Altus, Fort Supply, and Keystone. These areas are very good for many species of birds such as ducks and egrets.

Not only does Oklahoma have varying habitats, it has variations in the weather. Since the state extends over 400 miles (644 km) from west to east, weather ranges greatly. The Rocky Mountains to the west of Oklahoma form a moisture barrier, creating a rain shadow effect in western Oklahoma, making it much drier there. Eastern Oklahoma is much wetter and tends to be cooler. In the winter, it is not uncommon for those in southern Oklahoma to experience spring-like warm temperatures while it snows in the high elevations of the Panhandle.

No matter where you are in Oklahoma, there are birds to watch in every season. Whether witnessing a migration of hawks in the fall or welcoming back hummingbirds in spring, there is variety and excitement in birding as each season turns to the next.

OBSERVE WITH A STRATEGY: TIPS FOR IDENTIFYING BIRDS

Identifying birds isn't as difficult as you might think. By simply following a few basic strategies, you can increase your chances of successfully identifying most birds that you see. One of the first and easiest things to do when you see a new bird is to note **its color.** This field guide is organized by color, so simply turn to the right color section to find it.

Next, note the **size of the bird.** A strategy to quickly estimate size is to compare different birds. Pick a small, a medium, and a large bird. Select an American Robin as the medium bird. Measured from bill tip to tail tip, a robin is 10 inches (25 cm). Now select two other birds, one smaller and one larger. Good choices are a House Sparrow, at about 6 inches (15 cm), and an American Crow, around 18 inches (45 cm). When you see a species you don't know, you can now quickly ask yourself, "Is it larger than a sparrow but smaller than a robin?" When you look in your field guide to identify your bird, you would check the species that are roughly 6–10 inches (15–25 cm). This will help to narrow your choices.

Next, note the **size, shape, and color of the bill.** Is it long or short, thick or thin, pointed or blunt, curved or straight? Seed-eating birds, such as Northern Cardinals, have bills that are thick and strong enough to crack even the toughest seeds. Birds that sip nectar, such as Ruby-throated Hummingbirds, need long, thin bills to reach deep into flowers. Hawks and owls tear their prey with very sharp, curving bills. Sometimes, just noting the bill shape can help you decide whether the bird is a woodpecker, finch, grosbeak, blackbird, or bird of prey.

Next, take a look around and note the **habitat** in which you see the bird. Is it wading in a marsh? Walking along a riverbank or on the beach? Soaring in the sky? Is it perched high in the trees or hopping along the forest floor? Because of diet and habitat preferences, you'll often see robins hopping on the ground but not usually eating seeds at a feeder. Or you'll see a Rose-breasted Grosbeak sitting on a tree branch but not climbing headfirst down the trunk, like a Red-breasted Nuthatch would.

Noticing **what the bird is eating** will give you another clue to help you identify the species. Feeding is a big part of any bird's life. Fully one-third of all bird activity revolves around searching for food, catching prey, and eating. While birds don't always follow all the rules of their diet, you can make some general assumptions. Northern Flickers, for instance, feed on ants and other insects, so you wouldn't expect to see them visiting a seed feeder. Other birds, such as Barn and Cliff Swallows, eat flying insects and spend hours swooping and diving to catch a meal.

Sometimes, you can identify a bird by **the way it perches.** Body posture can help you differentiate between an American Crow and a Red-tailed Hawk, for example. Crows lean forward over their feet on a branch, while hawks perch in a vertical position. Consider posture the next time you see an unidentified large bird in a tree.

Birds in flight are harder to identify, but noting the **wing size and shape** will help. Wing size is in direct proportion to body size, weight, and type of flight. Wing shape determines whether the bird flies fast and with precision, or slowly and less precisely. Barn Swallows, for instance, have short, pointed wings that slice through the air, enabling swift, accurate flight. Turkey Vultures have long, broad wings for soaring on warm updrafts. House Finches have short, rounded wings, helping them to flit through thick tangles of branches.

Some bird species have a unique **pattern of flight** that can help in identification. American Goldfinches fly in a distinctive undulating pattern that makes it look like they're riding a roller coaster.

While it's not easy to make all of these observations in the short time you often have to watch a "mystery" bird, practicing these identification methods will greatly expand your birding skills. To further improve your skills, seek the guidance of a more experienced birder who can answer your questions on the spot.

BIRD BASICS

It's easier to identify birds and communicate about them if you know the names of the different parts of a bird. For instance, it's more effective to use the word "crest" to indicate the set of extra-long feathers on top of a Northern Cardinal's head than to try to describe it.

The following illustration points out the basic parts of a bird. Because it is a composite of many birds, it shouldn't be confused with any actual bird.

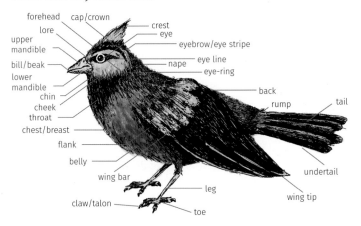

Bird Color Variables

No other animal has a color palette like a bird's. Brilliant blues, lemon yellows, showy reds, and iridescent greens are common in the bird world. In general, male birds are more colorful than their female counterparts. This helps males attract a mate, essentially saying, "Hey, look at me!" Color calls attention to a male's health as well. The better the condition of his feathers, the better his food source, territory, and potential for mating.

Male and female birds that don't look like each other are called sexually dimorphic, meaning "two forms." Dimorphic females often have a nondescript dull color, as seen in Rose-breasted Grosbeaks. Muted tones help females hide during the weeks of motionless incubation and draw less attention to them when they're out feeding or taking a break from the rigors of raising the young.

The males of some species, such as the Downy Woodpecker, Blue Jay and Bald Eagle, look nearly identical to the females. In woodpeckers, the sexes are differentiated by only a red mark, or sometimes a yellow mark. Depending on the species, the mark may be on top of the head, on the face or nape of neck, or just behind the bill.

During the first year, juvenile birds often look like their mothers. Since brightly colored feathers are used mainly for attracting a mate, young non-breeding males don't have a need for colorful plumage. It's not until the first spring molt (or several years later, depending on the species) that young males obtain their breeding colors.

Both breeding and winter plumages are the result of molting. Molting is the process of dropping old, worn feathers and replacing them with new ones. All birds molt, typically twice a year, with the spring molt usually occurring in late winter. At this time, most birds produce their brighter breeding plumage, which lasts throughout the summer.

Winter plumage is the result of the late summer molt, which serves a couple of important functions. First, it adds feathers for warmth in the coming winter season. Second, in some species, it produces feathers that tend to be drab in color, which helps to camouflage the birds and hide them from predators. The winter plumage of the male American Goldfinch, for example, is olive-brown, unlike its canary-yellow breeding color during summer. Luckily for us, some birds, such as the male Northern Cardinal, retain their bright summer colors all year long.

Bird Nests

Bird nests are a true feat of engineering. Imagine constructing a home that's strong enough to weather storms, large enough to hold your entire family, insulated enough to shelter them from cold and heat, and waterproof enough to keep out rain. Think about building it without blueprints or directions and using mainly your feet. Birds do this!

Before building, birds must select an appropriate site. In some species, such as the Bewick's Wren, the male picks out several potential sites and assembles small twigs in each. The "extra" nests, called dummy nests, discourage other birds from using any nearby cavities for their nests. The male takes the female around and shows her the choices. After choosing her favorite, she finishes the construction.

In other species, such as the Baltimore Oriole, the female selects the site and builds the nest, while the male offers an occasional suggestion. Each bird species has its own nest-building routine that is strictly followed.

As you can see in these illustrations, birds build a wide variety of nest types.

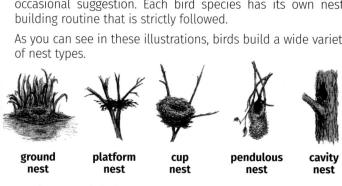

ground nest   **platform nest**   **cup nest**   **pendulous nest**   **cavity nest**

Nesting material often consists of natural items found in the immediate area. Most nests consist of plant fibers (such as bark from grapevines), sticks, mud, dried grass, feathers, fur, or soft, fuzzy tufts from thistle. Some birds, including Ruby-throated Hummingbirds, use spiderwebs to glue nest materials together.

Transportation of nesting material is limited to the amount a bird can hold or carry. Birds must make many trips afield to gather enough material to complete a nest. Most nests take four days or more and hundreds, if not thousands, of trips to build.

A **ground nest** can be a mound of vegetation on the ground or in the water. It can also be just a simple, shallow depression scraped out in earth, stones, or sand. Killdeer and Horned Larks scrape out ground nests without adding any nesting material.

The **platform nest** represents a much more complex type of construction. Typically built with twigs or sticks and branches, this nest forms a platform and has a depression in the center to nestle the eggs. Platform nests can be in trees; on balconies, cliffs, bridges, or man-made platforms; and even in flowerpots. They often provide space for the adventurous young and function as a landing platform for the parents.

Mourning Doves and herons don't anchor their platform nests to trees, so these can tumble from branches during high winds and storms. Hawks, eagles, ospreys and other birds construct sturdier platform nests with large sticks and branches.

Other platform nests are constructed on the ground with mud, grass, and other vegetation from the area. Many waterfowl build platform nests on the ground near or in water. A **floating platform nest** moves with the water level, preventing the nest, eggs, and birds from being flooded.

Three-quarters of all songbirds construct a **cup nest,** which is a modified platform nest. The supporting platform is built first and attached firmly to a tree, shrub, or rock ledge or the ground. Next, the sides are constructed with grass, small twigs, bark, or leaves, which are woven together and often glued with mud for added strength. The inner cup can be lined with down feathers, animal fur or hair, or soft plant materials and is contoured last.

The **pendulous nest** is an unusual nest that looks like a sock hanging from a branch. Attached to the end of small branches of trees, this unique nest is inaccessible to most predators and often waves wildly in a breeze.

Woven tightly with plant fibers, the pendulous nest is strong and watertight and takes up to a week to build. A small opening at the top or on the side allows parents access to the grass-lined interior. More commonly used by tropical birds, this complex nest has also been mastered by orioles and kinglets. It must be one heck of a ride to be inside one of these nests during a windy spring thunderstorm!

The **cavity nest** is used by many species of birds, most notably woodpeckers and Eastern Bluebirds. A cavity nest is often excavated from a branch or tree trunk and offers shelter from storms, sun, cold, and predators. A small entrance hole in a tree can lead to a nest chamber that is up to a safe 10 inches (25 cm) deep.

Typically made by woodpeckers, cavity nests are usually used only once by the builder. Nest cavities can be used for many subsequent years by such inhabitants as Wood Ducks, mergansers, and bluebirds. Kingfishers, on the other hand, can dig a tunnel up to 4 feet (about 1 m) long in a riverbank. The nest chamber at the end of the tunnel is already well insulated, so it's usually only sparsely lined.

One of the most clever of all nests is the **no nest,** or daycare nest. Parasitic birds, such as Brown-headed Cowbirds, don't build their own nests. Instead, the egg-laden female searches out the nest of another bird and sneaks in to lay an egg while the host mother isn't looking.

A mother cowbird wastes no energy building a nest only to have it raided by a predator. Laying her eggs in the nests of other birds transfers the responsibility of raising her young to the host. When she lays her eggs in several nests, the chances increase that at least one of her babies will live to maturity.

Who Builds the Nest?

Generally, the female bird constructs the nest. She gathers the materials and does the building, with an occasional visit from her mate to check on progress. In some species, both parents contribute equally to nest building. The male may forage for sticks, grass, or mud, but it is the female that often fashions the nest. Only rarely does a male build a nest by himself.

Fledging

Fledging is the time between hatching and flight or leaving the nest. Some species of birds are **precocial,** meaning they leave the nest within hours of hatching, though it may be weeks before they can fly. This is common in waterfowl and shorebirds.

Baby birds that hatch naked and blind need to stay in the nest for a few weeks (these birds are **altricial**). Baby birds that are still in the nest are **nestlings.** Until birds start to fly, they are called **fledglings.**

Why Birds Migrate

Why do so many species of birds migrate? The short answer is simple: food. Birds migrate to locations with abundant food, as it is easier to breed where there is food than where food is scarce. Rose-breasted Grosbeaks, for instance, are **complete migrators** that fly from the tropics of Central and South America to nest in the forests of North America, where billions of newly hatched insects are available to feed to their young.

Other migrators, such as some birds of prey, migrate back to northern regions in spring. In these locations, they hunt mice, voles, and other small rodents that are beginning to breed.

Complete migrators have a set time and pattern of migration. Every year, at nearly the same time, they head to a specific wintering ground. Complete migrators may travel great distances, sometimes 15,000 miles (24,100 km) or more in one year.

Complete migration doesn't necessarily imply flying from the cold, frozen northland to a tropical destination. The Dark-eyed Junco, for example, is a complete migrator that flies from the far reaches of Canada to spend the winter right here in Oklahoma. This trip is still considered complete migration.

Complete migrators have many interesting aspects. In spring, males often leave a few weeks before the females, arriving early to scope out possibilities for nesting sites and food sources, and to begin defending territories. The females arrive several weeks later. In many species, the females and their young leave earlier in the fall, often up to four weeks before the adult males.

Other species, such as the American Goldfinch, are **partial migrators**. These birds usually wait until their food supplies dwindle before flying south. Unlike complete migrators, partial migrators move only far enough south, or sometimes east and west, to find abundant food. In some years it might be only a few hundred miles, while in other years, it can be as much as a thousand. This kind of migration, dependent on weather and the availability of food, is sometimes called seasonal movement.

Unlike the predictable complete migrators or partial migrators, **irruptive migrators** can move every third to fifth year or, in some cases, in consecutive years. These migrations are triggered when times are tough, and food is scarce. Red-breasted Nuthatches are irruptive migrators. They leave their normal northern range in search of more food or in response to overpopulation.

Many other birds don't migrate at all. Black-capped Chickadees, for example, are **non-migrators** that remain in their habitat all year long and just move around as necessary to find food.

How Do Birds Migrate?

One of the many secrets of migration is fat. While most people are fighting the ongoing battle of the bulge, birds intentionally gorge themselves to gain as much fat as possible without losing the ability to fly. Fat provides the greatest amount of energy per unit of weight. In the same way that your car needs gas, birds are propelled by fat and stall without it.

During long migratory flights, fat deposits are used up quickly, and birds need to stop to refuel. This is when backyard bird feeding stations and undeveloped, natural spaces around our towns and cities are especially important. Some birds require up to 2–3 days of constant feeding to build their fat reserves before continuing their seasonal trip.

Many birds, such as most eagles, hawks, falcons, and vultures, migrate during the day. Larger birds can hold more body fat, go longer without eating, and take longer to migrate. These birds glide along on rising columns of warm air, called thermals, that hold them aloft while they slowly make their way north or south. They generally rest at night and hunt early in the morning before the sun has a chance to warm the land and create good soaring conditions. Daytime migrators use a combination of landforms, rivers, and the rising and setting sun to guide them in the right direction.

The majority of small birds, called **passerines,** migrate at night. Studies show that some use the stars to navigate. Others use the setting sun, and still others, such as doves, use Earth's magnetic field to guide them north or south.

While flying at night may not seem like a good idea, it's actually safer. First, there are fewer avian predators hunting for birds at night. Second, night travel allows time during the day to find food in unfamiliar surroundings. Third, wind patterns at night tend to be flat, or laminar. Flat winds don't have the turbulence of daytime winds and can help push the smaller birds along.

HOW TO USE THIS GUIDE

To help you quickly and easily identify birds, this field guide is organized by color. Refer to the color key on the first page, note the color of the bird, and turn to that section. For example, the male Rose-breasted Grosbeak is black and white with a red patch on its chest. Because the bird is mostly black and white, it will be found in the black-and-white section.

Each color section is also arranged by size, generally with the smaller birds first. Sections may also incorporate the average size in a range, which in some cases reflects size differences between male and female birds. Flip through the pages in the color section to find the bird. If you already know the name of the bird, check the index for the page number.

In some species, the male and female are very different in color. In others, the breeding and winter plumage colors differ. These species will have an inset photograph with a page reference and will be found in two color sections.

You will find a variety of information in the bird description sections. To learn more, turn to the sample on pp. 22–23.

Range Maps

Range maps are included for each bird. Colored areas indicate where the bird is frequently found. The colors represent the presence of a species during a specific season, not the density or amount of birds in the area. Green is used for summer, blue for winter, red for year-round and yellow for migration.

While every effort has been made to depict accurate ranges, these are constantly in flux due to a variety of factors. Changing weather, habitat, species abundance, and availability of vital resources, such as food and water, can affect the migration and movement of local populations, causing birds to be found in areas that are atypical for the species. So please use the maps as intended—as general guides only.

female
p. 103

male

Common Name

Range Map   *Scientific name*   **Color Indicator**

Size: measurement is from head to tip of tail; wingspan may be listed as well

Male: brief description of the male bird; may include breeding, winter, or other plumages

Female: brief description of the female bird, which is sometimes different from the male

Juvenile: brief description of the juvenile bird, which often looks like the adult female

Nest: kind of nest the bird builds to raise its young; who builds it; number of broods per year

Eggs: number of eggs you might expect to see in a nest; color and marking

Incubation: average days the parents spend incubating the eggs; who does the incubation

Fledging: average days the young spend in the nest after hatching but before they leave the nest; who does the most "childcare" and feeding

Migration: type of migrator: complete (seasonal, consistent), partial (seasonal, destination varies), irruptive (unpredictable, depends on the food supply), or non-migrator

Food: what the bird eats most of the time (e.g., seeds, insects, fruit, nectar, small mammals, fish) and whether it typically comes to a bird feeder

Compare: notes about other birds that look similar and the pages on which they can be found; may include extra information to aid in identification

Stan's Notes: Interesting natural history information. This could be something to look or listen for or something to help positively identify the bird. Also includes remarkable features.

female
p. 131

male

Brown-headed Cowbird

Molothrus ater

Size: 7½" (19 cm)

Male: Glossy black with a chocolate-brown head. Dark eyes. Pointed, sharp gray bill.

Female: dull brown with a pointed, sharp, gray bill

Juvenile: similar to female but with dull-gray plumage and a streaked chest

Nest: no nest; lays eggs in nests of other birds

Eggs: 5–7; white with brown markings

Incubation: 10–13 days; host birds incubate eggs

Fledging: 10–11 days; host birds feed the young

Migration: non-migrator in Oklahoma

Food: insects, seeds; will come to seed feeders

Compare: The male Red-winged Blackbird (p. 31) is slightly larger with red-and-yellow patches on upper wings. Common Grackle (p. 35) has a long tail and lacks the brown head. European Starling (p. 27) has a shorter tail.

Stan's Notes: Cowbirds are members of the blackbird family. Of approximately 750 species of parasitic birds worldwide, this is the only parasitic bird in Oklahoma. Brood parasites lay their eggs in the nests of other birds, leaving the host birds to raise their young. Cowbirds are known to have laid their eggs in the nests of over 200 species of birds. While some birds reject cowbird eggs, most incubate them and raise the young, even to the exclusion of their own. Look for warblers and other birds feeding young birds twice their own size. Named "Cowbird" for its habit of following bison and cattle herds to feed on insects flushed up by the animals.

winter

breeding

European Starling
Sturnus vulgaris

Size: 7½" (19 cm)

Male: Glittering, iridescent purplish black in spring and summer; duller and speckled with white in fall and winter. Long, pointed, yellow bill in spring; gray in fall. Pointed wings. Short tail.

Female: same as male

Juvenile: similar to adults, with grayish-brown plumage and a streaked chest

Nest: cavity; male and female line cavity; 2 broods per year

Eggs: 4–6; bluish with brown markings

Incubation: 12–14 days; female and male incubate

Fledging: 18–20 days; female and male feed the young

Migration: non-migrator to partial migrator; some will move to southern states

Food: insects, seeds, fruit; visits seed or suet feeders

Compare: The Common Grackle (p. 35) has a long tail. Male Brown-headed Cowbird (p. 25) has a brown head. Look for the shiny, dark feathers to help identify the European Starling.

Stan's Notes: One of our most numerous songbirds. Mimics the songs of up to 20 bird species and imitates sounds, including the human voice. Jaws are more powerful when opening than when closing, enabling the bird to pry open crevices to find insects. Often displaces woodpeckers, chickadees, and other cavity-nesting birds. Large families gather with blackbirds in the fall. Not a native bird; 100 starlings were introduced to New York City in 1890–91 from Europe. Bill changes color in spring and fall.

female
p. 143

Eastern
Towhee

Spotted Towhee
Pipilo maculatus

WINTER

Size: 8½" (22 cm)

Male: Mostly black with dirty red-brown sides and a white belly. Multiple white spots on wings and sides. Long black tail with a white tip. Rich, red eyes.

Female: very similar to male but with a brown head

Juvenile: brown with a heavily streaked chest

Nest: cup; female builds; 1–2 broods per year

Eggs: 3–5; white with brown markings

Incubation: 12–14 days; female and male incubate

Fledging: 10–12 days; female and male feed young

Migration: partial to non-migrator; winters in Oklahoma

Food: seeds, fruit, insects

Compare: American Robin (p. 231) is larger. Male Rose-breasted Grosbeak (p. 51) has a rosy patch in center of chest.

Stan's Notes: Once considered a single species, Spotted Towhee and Eastern Towhee were knows as Rufous-sided Towhee. Spotted Towhees are seen throughout Oklahoma, while Eastern Towhees are found in the eastern part of the state. Found in a variety of habitats from thick brush and forest edges to suburban backyards. Usually heard noisily scratching through dead leaves on the ground for food. Over 70 percent of its diet is plant material. Eats more insects during spring and summer. Well known to retreat from danger by walking away rather than taking to flight. Nest is nearly always on the ground under bushes but away from where the male perches to sing. Song and plumage vary geographically and aren't well studied or understood.

female
p. 141

male

Red-winged Blackbird
Agelaius phoeniceus

YEAR-ROUND

Size: 8½" (22 cm)

Male: Jet black with red-and-yellow patches (epaulets) on upper wings. Pointed black bill.

Female: heavily streaked brown with a pointed brown bill and white eyebrows

Juvenile: same as female

Nest: cup; female builds; 2–3 broods per year

Eggs: 3–4; bluish green with brown markings

Incubation: 10–12 days; female incubates

Fledging: 11–14 days; female and male feed the young

Migration: non-migrator to partial migrator

Food: seeds, insects; visits seed and suet feeders

Compare: Male Brown-headed Cowbird (p. 25) is smaller and glossier and has a brown head. The bold red-and-yellow epaulets distinguish the male Red-winged from other blackbirds.

Stan's Notes: One of the most widespread and numerous birds in Oklahoma. Found around marshes, wetlands, lakes, and rivers. Flocks with as many as 10,000 birds have been reported. Males arrive before the females and sing to defend their territory. The male repeats his call from the top of a cattail while showing off his red-and-yellow shoulder patches. The female chooses a mate and often builds her nest over shallow water in a thick stand of cattails. The male can be aggressive when defending the nest. Red-winged Blackbirds feed mostly on seeds in spring and fall, and insects throughout the summer.

female
p. 151

male

Yellow-headed Blackbird

Xanthocephalus xanthocephalus

SUMMER MIGRATION

Size: 9–11" (23–28 cm)

Male: Large black bird with a lemon-yellow head, breast, and nape of neck. Black mask and gray bill. White wing patches.

Female: similar to male but slightly smaller with a brown body and dull-yellow head and chest

Juvenile: similar to female

Nest: cup; female builds; 2 broods per year

Eggs: 3–5; greenish white with brown markings

Incubation: 11–13 days; female incubates

Fledging: 9–12 days; female feeds the young

Migration: complete, to southern states and Mexico

Food: insects, seeds; will come to ground feeders

Compare: The male Red-winged Blackbird (p. 31) is smaller and has red-and-yellow patches on its wings. Look for the bright-yellow head to identify the male Yellow-headed.

Stan's Notes: Found around marshes, wetlands, and lakes. Nests in deep water, unlike its cousin, the Red-winged Blackbird, which prefers shallow water. Usually heard before seen. Gives a raspy, low, metallic-sounding call. The male is the only large black bird with a bright-yellow head. He gives an impressive mating display, flying with his head drooped and feet and tail pointing down while steadily beating his wings. Young keep low and out of sight for up to three weeks before they start to fly. Migrates in large flocks of as many as 200 birds, often with Red-winged Blackbirds and Brown-headed Cowbirds. Flocks of mainly males return in late March and early April; females return later. Most colonies consist of 20–100 nests.

33

Common Grackle
Quiscalus quiscula

Size: 11–13" (28–33 cm)

Male: Large, iridescent blackbird with bluish-black head and purplish-brown body. Long black tail. Long, thin bill and bright-golden eyes.

Female: similar to male but smaller and duller

Juvenile: similar to female

Nest: cup; female builds; 2 broods per year

Eggs: 4–5; greenish white with brown markings

Incubation: 13–14 days; female incubates

Fledging: 16–20 days; female and male feed the young

Migration: non-migrator to partial in Oklahoma; will move around to find food

Food: fruit, seeds, insects; will come to seed and suet feeders

Compare: Male Great-tailed Grackle (p. 39) is larger and has a much longer tail. The European Starling (p. 27) is much smaller with a speckled appearance, and a yellow bill during breeding season. Male Red-winged Blackbird (p. 31) has red-and-yellow wing markings (epaulets).

Stan's Notes: Usually nests in small colonies of up to 75 pairs but travels with other blackbird species in large flocks. Known to feed in farm fields. The common name is derived from the Latin word *gracula*, meaning "jackdaw," another species of bird and a term that can refer to any bird in the *Quiscalus* genus. The male holds his tail in a deep V shape during flight. The flight pattern is usually level, as opposed to an undulating movement. Unlike most birds, it has larger muscles for opening its mouth than for closing it, enabling it to pry crevices apart to find hidden insects.

American Coot
Fulica americana

Size: 13–16" (33–40 cm)

Male: Gray-to-black waterbird. Duck-like white bill with a dark band near the tip and a small red patch near the eyes. Small white patch near base of tail. Green legs and feet. Red eyes.

Female: same as male

Juvenile: much paler than adults, with a gray bill

Nest: floating platform; female and male construct; 1 brood per year

Eggs: 9–12; pinkish buff with brown markings

Incubation: 21–25 days; female and male incubate

Fledging: 49–52 days; female and male feed young

Migration: non-migrator to partial in Oklahoma

Food: insects, aquatic plants

Compare: Smaller than most waterfowl, it is the only black, duck-like bird with a white bill.

Stan's Notes: Usually seen in large flocks on open water. Not a duck, as it has large lobed toes instead of webbed feet. An excellent diver and swimmer, bobbing its head as it swims. A favorite food of Bald Eagles. It is not often seen in flight, unless it's trying to escape from an eagle. To take off, it scrambles across the surface of the water, flapping its wings. Gives a unique series of creaks, groans, and clicks. Anchors its floating platform nest to vegetation. Huge flocks with as many as 1,000 birds gather for migration. Migrates at night. The common name "Coot" comes from the Middle English word *coote*, which was used to describe various waterfowl. Also called Mud Hen.

female
p. 169

male

Great-tailed Grackle
Quiscalus mexicanus

Size: 18" (45 cm), male
15" (38 cm), female

Male: Large all-black bird with iridescent purple sheen on the head and back. Exceptionally long tail. Bright-yellow eyes.

Female: much smaller than the male, brown bird with gray to brown belly, light-brown-to-white eyes, eyebrows, throat, and upper chest.

Juvenile: similar to female

Nest: cup; female builds; 1–2 broods per year

Eggs: 3–5; greenish blue with brown markings

Incubation: 12–14 days; female incubates

Fledging: 21–23 days; female feeds the young

Migration: non-migrator to partial migrator; moves around to find food

Food: insects, fruit, seeds; comes to seed feeders

Compare: Common Grackle (p. 35) is smaller, with a much shorter tail. Male Brown-headed Cowbird (p. 25) lacks the long tail and has a brown head.

Stan's Notes: This is our largest grackle. It was once considered a subspecies of the Boat-tailed Grackle, which occurs along the East Coast and Florida. Prefers to nest close to water in an open habitat. A colony nester. Males do not participate in nest building, incubation, or raising young. Males rarely fight; females squabble over nest sites and materials. Several females mate with one male. They are expanding northward, moving into northern states. Western populations tend to be larger than the eastern. Song varies from population to population.

in flight

American Crow
Corvus brachyrhynchos

YEAR-ROUND

Size: 18" (45 cm)

Male: All-black bird with black bill, legs, and feet. Can have a purple sheen in direct sunlight.

Female: same as male

Juvenile: same as adult

Nest: platform; female builds; 1 brood per year

Eggs: 4–6; bluish to olive-green with brown marks

Incubation: 18 days; female incubates

Fledging: 28–35 days; female and male feed the young

Migration: non-migrator; moves around in winter

Food: fruit, insects, mammals, fish, carrion; will come to seed and suet feeders

Compare: Black-billed Magpie (p. 67) has a long tail and white belly. Smaller than Chihuahuan Raven (not shown), has a smaller bill and lacks shaggy throat feathers. The Crow has a higher-pitched call than Raven's deep, low raspy call. Crow has a squared tail. Raven has a wedge-shaped tail, apparent in flight.

Stan's Notes: One of the most recognizable birds in Oklahoma, found in most habitats. Imitates other birds and human voices. One of the smartest of all birds and very social, often entertaining itself by provoking chases with other birds. Eats roadkill but is rarely hit by vehicles. Can live as long as 20 years. Often reuses its nest every year if it's not taken over by a Great Horned Owl. Unmated birds, known as helpers, help to raise the young. Extended families roost together at night, dispersing daily to hunt. Cannot soar on thermals; flaps constantly and glides downward. Gathers in huge communal flocks of up to 10,000 birds in winter.

soaring

juvenile

drying

Turkey Vulture
Cathartes aura

Size: 26–32" (66–80 cm); up to 6' wingspan

Male: Large and black with a naked red head and legs. In flight, wings are two-toned with a black leading edge and a gray trailing edge. Wing tips end in finger-like projections. Tail is long and squared. Ivory bill.

Female: same as male but slightly smaller

Juvenile: similar to adults, with a gray-to-blackish head and bill

Nest: no nest or minimal nest, on a cliff or in a cave, sometimes in a hollow tree; 1 brood per year

Eggs: 1–3; white with brown markings

Incubation: 38–41 days; female and male incubate

Fledging: 66–88 days; female and male feed the young

Migration: complete, to southern states, Mexico, and Central and South America; non-migrator in parts of Oklahoma

Food: carrion; parents regurgitate to feed the young

Compare: Bald Eagle (p. 71) is larger and lacks two-toned wings. Look for the obvious naked red head to identify the Turkey Vulture.

Stan's Notes: The naked head reduces the risk of feather fouling (picking up diseases) from contact with carcasses. It has a strong bill for tearing apart flesh. Unlike hawks and eagles, it has weak feet more suited for walking than grasping. One of the few birds with a developed sense of smell. Mostly mute, making only grunts and groans. Holds its wings in an upright V shape in flight. Teeters from wing tip to wing tip as it soars and hovers. Seen in trees with wings outstretched, sunning itself and drying after a rain.

in flight

juvenile

crests

drying

Double-crested Cormorant

Phalacrocorax auritus

Size: 31–35" (79–89 cm); up to 4⅓' wingspan

Male: Large black waterbird with unusual blue eyes and a long, snakelike neck. Large gray bill, with yellow at the base and a hooked tip.

Female: same as male

Juvenile: lighter brown with a grayish chest and neck

Nest: platform; male and female construct; 1 brood per year

Eggs: 3–4; bluish white without markings

Incubation: 25–29 days; female and male incubate

Fledging: 37–42 days; male and female feed the young

Migration: complete, to southern states, Mexico, and Central America; winters in Oklahoma

Food: small fish, aquatic insects

Compare: The Turkey Vulture (p. 43) also spreads out its wings to dry in the sun, but it has a naked red head. The American Coot (p. 37) has a duck-like white bill. Look for the long, snakelike neck and large, hooked bill to help identify the Cormorant.

Stan's Notes: Flies in a large V or a line. Usually roosts in large colonies in trees close to water. Swims underwater to catch fish, holding its wings at its sides. This bird's outer feathers soak up water, but its body feathers don't. To dry off, it strikes an upright pose with wings outstretched, facing the sun. Gives grunts, pops, and groans. Named "Double-crested" for the crests on its head, which are not often seen. "Cormorant" is a contraction from *corvus marinus*, meaning "crow" or "raven," and "of the sea."

male

female

Downy Woodpecker
Dryobates pubescens

YEAR-ROUND

Size: 6½" (15 cm)

Male: Small woodpecker with a white belly and black-and-white spotted wings. Red mark on the back of the head and a white stripe down the back. Short black bill.

Female: same as male but lacks the red mark

Juvenile: same as female, some with a red mark near the forehead

Nest: cavity with a round entrance hole; male and female excavate; 1 brood per year

Eggs: 3–5; white without markings

Incubation: 11–12 days; female incubates during the day, male incubates at night

Fledging: 20–25 days; male and female feed the young

Migration: non-migrator

Food: insects, seeds; visits seed and suet feeders

Compare: The Hairy Woodpecker (p. 53) is larger. Look for the Downy's shorter, thinner bill.

Stan's Notes: Abundant and widespread where trees are present and perhaps the most common woodpecker in the United States. Stiff tail feathers help to brace it like a tripod as it clings to a tree. Like other woodpeckers, it has a long, barbed tongue to pull insects from tiny places. Mates drum on branches or hollow logs to announce territory, which is rarely larger than 5 acres (2 ha). Repeats a high-pitched "peek-peek" call. Male performs most of the brooding. During winter, it will roost in a cavity. Undulates in flight.

female
p. 115

breeding male

non-breeding
male

Lark Bunting
Calamospiza melanocorys

Size: 6½" (16 cm)

Male: Short, stocky black bird with a large, broad head. White wing patches and large bluish-gray bill. Winter male is black, brown, gray and white-striped with white wing patches.

Female: overall brown with a heavily streaked chest, white belly, black vertical line on each side of white chin, may have a dark central spot on the chest, faint white eyebrows

Juvenile: similar to adult of the same sex

Nest: cup; female builds; 1–2 broods per year

Eggs: 4–6; pale blue with markings

Incubation: 11–13 days; female and male incubate

Fledging: 8–12 days; female and male feed young

Migration: complete, to southwestern states; non-migrator in parts of Oklahoma

Food: insects, seeds

Compare: The breeding male's bold black-and-white plumage is hard to confuse with any other bird's. Look for the rather large broad head and large bill to help identify.

Stan's Notes: Common in western Oklahoma in dry plains and sagebrush regions. Has short, rounded wings. Flying with shallow wingbeats, the male flashes white wing patches. Male takes to air to display to female, setting its wings in a V position and floating back, rocking like a butterfly, singing a most amazing song. Song is like the song of Old World larks, hence the common name. Will flock in fall with hundreds, if not thousands, of other Lark Buntings for migration.

female
p. 127

male

Rose-breasted Grosbeak
Pheucticus ludovicianus

Size: 7–8" (18–20 cm)

Male: Plump black-and-white bird with a large triangular, rose-colored patch on the breast. Wing linings are rose red. Large ivory bill.

Female: heavily streaked with obvious white eyebrows and orange-to-yellow wing linings

Juvenile: similar to female

Nest: cup; female and male construct; 1–2 broods per year

Eggs: 3–5; blue-green with brown markings

Incubation: 13–14 days; female and male incubate

Fledging: 9–12 days; female and male feed the young

Migration: complete, to Mexico, Central America, and South America

Food: insects, seeds, fruit; comes to seed feeders

Compare: Male is very distinctive, with no look-alikes. Look for the rose breast patch to identify.

Stan's Notes: Seen throughout Oklahoma during spring and autumn migrations. Small summer resident population in parts of Oklahoma. Prefers a mature deciduous forest for nesting. Both sexes sing, but the male sings much louder and clearer. Sings a rich, robin-like song with a chip note in the tune. "Grosbeak" refers to the thick, strong bill, which is used to crush seeds. The rose patch varies in size and shape in each male. Males have white wing patches that flash during flight. Males arrive at the breeding grounds a few days before the females. Late to arrive in spring and early to leave in autumn. Often prefers mature deciduous forest for nesting. Doesn't nest in Oklahoma.

male

female

Hairy Woodpecker
Leuconotopicus villosus

Size: 9" (23 cm)

Male: Black-and-white woodpecker with a white belly. Black wings with rows of white spots. White stripe down the back. Long black bill. Red mark on the back of the head.

Female: same as male but lacks the red mark

Juvenile: grayer version of the female

Nest: cavity with an oval entrance hole; female and male excavate; 1 brood per year

Eggs: 3–6; white without markings

Incubation: 11–15 days; female incubates during the day, male incubates at night

Fledging: 28–30 days; male and female feed the young

Migration: non-migrator; moves around in winter to find food

Food: insects, nuts, seeds; comes to seed and suet feeders

Compare: Downy Woodpecker (p. 47) is much smaller and has a much shorter bill. Look for Hairy Woodpecker's long bill.

Stan's Notes: A common bird in wooded backyards. Announces its arrival with a sharp chirp before landing on feeders. Responsible for eating many destructive forest insects. Uses its barbed tongue to extract insects from trees. Tiny, bristle-like feathers at the base of the bill protect the nostrils from wood dust. Drums on hollow logs, branches, or stovepipes in spring to announce territory. Prefers to excavate nest cavities in live aspen trees. Excavates a larger, more oval-shaped entrance than the round entrance hole of the Downy Woodpecker. Makes short flights from tree to tree.

juvenile

Red-headed Woodpecker
Melanerpes erythrocephalus

YEAR-ROUND
SUMMER

Size: 9" (22.5 cm)

Male: All-red head with a solid black back. White chest, belly, and rump. Black wings with large white wing patches seen flashing in flight. Black tail. Gray legs and bill.

Female: same as male

Juvenile: gray brown with white chest, lacks any red

Nest: cavity; male builds with help from female; 1 brood per year

Eggs: 4–5; white without markings

Incubation: 12–13 days; female and male incubate

Fledging: 27–30 days; female and male feed the young

Migration: partial migrator to non-migrator; will move to areas with an abundant supply of nuts

Food: insects, nuts, fruit; visits suet and seed feeders

Compare: No other woodpecker in Oklaholma has an all-red head. Pileated Woodpecker (p. 65) is the only other woodpecker with a solid black back, but it has a partial red head.

Stan's Notes: One of the few non-dimorphic woodpeckers, with males and females that look alike. Bill is strong enough to excavate a nest cavity only in soft, dead trees. Prefers open woodlands or woodland edges with many dead or rotting branches. Unlike other woodpeckers, which use nest cavities just once briefly, it may use the same cavity for several years in a row. Often perches on top of dead snags. Stores acorns and other nuts. Gives a shrill, hoarse "churr" call. Was once the most common of woodpeckers and now is very uncommon to rare. Population decline over 90 percent.

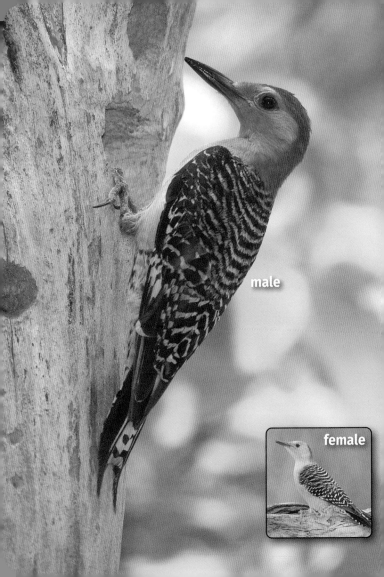

male

female

Red-bellied Woodpecker
Melanerpes carolinus

Size: 9–9½" (23–24 cm)

Male: Black-and-white "zebra-backed" woodpecker with a white rump. Red crown extends down the nape of the neck. Tan chest. Pale-red tinge on the belly, often hard to see.

Female: same as male but with a light-gray crown and a red nape

Juvenile: gray version of adults; lacks a red crown and red nape

Nest: cavity; female and male excavate; 1 brood per year

Eggs: 4–5; white without markings

Incubation: 12–14 days; female incubates during the day, male incubates at night

Fledging: 24–27 days; female and male feed the young

Migration: non-migrator; moves around to find food

Food: insects, nuts, fruit; visits suet and seed feeders

Compare: Similar to the Northern Flicker (p. 161). The Red-headed Woodpecker (p. 55) has an all-red head. Look for the zebra-striped back to help identify the Red-bellied Woodpecker.

Stan's Notes: Likes shady woodlands, forest edges, and backyards. Digs holes in rotten wood to find spiders, centipedes, beetles, and more. Hammers acorns and berries into crevices of trees for winter food. Returns to the same tree to excavate a new nest below that of the previous year. Often kicked out of nest hole by European Starlings. Undulating flight with rapid wingbeats. Gives a loud "querrr" call and a low "chug-chug-chug." Named for the pale red tinge on its belly. Expanding its range all over the country.

female

male

Scissor-tailed Flycatcher
Tyrannus forficatus

SUMMER

Size: 10" (24 cm)

Male: White-to-gray head, neck, breast, and back. Black wings with bright pink wing linings, seen in flight. Faint pink coloring on flanks and belly. An extremely long black tail with patches of white.

Female: similar to male, with a much shorter tail

Juvenile: similar to adults, with a shorter tail, lacking pink underwings and sides

Nest: cup; female builds; 1 brood per year

Eggs: 3–5; white with brown and red markings

Incubation: 14–17 days; female incubates

Fledging: 14–16 days; female and male feed young

Migration: complete, to Central and South America

Food: insects

Compare: This flycatcher's extremely long tail and the distinctive black-and-white pattern with its pink wing linings make it hard to confuse with any other bird.

Stan's Notes: A wonderful summer resident. Like most flycatchers, it hunts for insects by waiting on a post or low tree and flying out to capture them as they pass by. Drops to the ground to hunt for insects much more than other flycatchers. Male performs an up-down and zigzag courtship flight, showing off his long tail. Sometimes will end the flight with a reverse somersault. When not breeding, often seen in large flocks. Roosts communally, with up to 200 individuals. Closely related to kingbirds.

female p.175

male

Lesser Scaup
Aythya affinis

WINTER

Size: 16–17" (40–43 cm)

Male: Appears mostly black with bold white sides and a gray back. Chest and head look nearly black, but head appears purple with green highlights in direct sun. Bright-yellow eyes.

Female: overall brown with a dull-white patch at the base of a light-gray bill; yellow eyes

Juvenile: same as female

Nest: ground; female builds; 1 brood per year

Eggs: 8–14; olive-buff without markings

Incubation: 22–28 days; female incubates

Fledging: 45–50 days; female teaches the young to feed

Migration: complete, to southern states, Mexico, Central America, and northern South America

Food: aquatic plants and insects

Compare: Larger than American Coot (p. 37), which lacks male Scaup's white sides. The male Blue-winged Teal (p. 173) is slightly smaller, with a white crescent on its bill. The white sides and gray back help identify the male Lesser Scaup.

Stan's Notes: A common wintering duck in the state. Often seen in large flocks on lakes, ponds, and sewage lagoons during migration and winter. A common diving duck. Submerges completely to feed on the bottom (unlike dabbling ducks, which tip forward to reach the bottom). Note the bold white stripe under the wings when in flight. The male leaves the female when she starts incubating eggs. Egg quantity (clutch size) increases with the female's age. Has an interesting babysitting arrangement: groups of young (crèches) are tended by one to three adult females.

winter

breeding

American Avocet
Recurvirostra americana

SUMMER
MIGRATION

Size: 18" (45 cm)

Male: Black-and-white back, with a white belly. A long, thin, upturned bill and long gray legs. Rusty-red head and neck during breeding season, gray in winter.

Female: similar to male, more strongly upturned bill

Juvenile: similar to adults, slight wash of rusty red on the neck and head

Nest: ground; female and male construct; 1 brood per year

Eggs: 3–5; light olive with brown markings

Incubation: 22–29 days; female and male incubate

Fledging: 28–35 days; female and male feed young

Migration: complete, to southwestern states, Mexico

Food: insects, crustaceans, aquatic vegetation, fruit

Compare: One of the few long-legged shorebirds in Oklahoma. Look for the rusty-red head of breeding Avocet and the long upturned bill.

Stan's Notes: A handsome, long-legged bird that prefers shallow alkaline, saline, or brackish water, it is well adapted to arid western U.S. conditions. Uses its upturned bill to sweep from side to side across mud bottoms in search of insects. Both the male and female have a brood patch to incubate eggs and brood their young. Nests in western Oklahoma in loose colonies of up to 20 pairs; all members defend against intruders together.

male

female

Pileated Woodpecker
Dryocopus pileatus

YEAR-ROUND

Size: 19" (48 cm)

Male: Crow-size woodpecker with a black back and bright-red forehead, crest, and mustache. Long gray bill. White leading edge of wings flashes brightly during flight.

Female: same as male but with a black forehead; lacks a red mustache

Juvenile: similar to adults but duller and browner

Nest: cavity; male and female excavate; 1 brood per year

Eggs: 3–5; white without markings

Incubation: 15–18 days; female incubates during the day, male incubates at night

Fledging: 26–28 days; female and male feed the young

Migration: non-migrator; moves around to find food

Food: insects; will come to suet and peanut feeders

Compare: The Red-headed Woodpecker (p. 55) is about half the size and has an all-red head. Look for the bright-red crest and exceptionally large size to identify the Pileated Woodpecker.

Stan's Notes: Our largest woodpecker. The common name comes from the Latin *pileatus*, which means "wearing a cap." A relatively shy bird that prefers large tracts of woodland. Drums on hollow branches, chimneys, and so forth to announce its territory. Excavates oval holes up to several feet long in tree trunks, looking for insects to eat. Large wood chips lie on the ground by excavated trees. Favorite food is carpenter ants. Feeds regurgitated insects to its young. Young emerge from the nest, looking just like the adults.

Black-billed Magpie
Pica hudsonia

Size: 20" (50 cm)

Male: Large black-and-white bird with a very long tail and white belly. Iridescent green wings and tail in direct sunlight. Large black bill. Black legs. White wing patches flash in flight.

Female: same as male

Juvenile: same as adult, but has a shorter tail

Nest: modified pendulous; male and female build; 1 brood per year

Eggs: 5–8; green with brown markings

Incubation: 16–21 days; female incubates

Fledging: 25–29 days; female and male feed young

Migration: non-migrator

Food: insects, carrion, fruit, seeds

Compare: Larger than the Common Grackle (p. 35). The contrasting black-and-white colors and the very long tail of the Black-billed Magpie distinguish it from the all-black American Crow (p. 41).

Stan's Notes: A wonderfully intelligent bird that is able to mimic dogs, cats, and even people. Will often raid a barnyard dog dish for food. Feeds on a variety of food, from roadkill to insects and seeds it collects from the ground. Easily identified by its bold black-and-white colors and long streaming tail. Travels in small flocks, usually family members, and tends to be very gregarious. Breeds in small colonies. Unusual dome nest (dome-shaped roof) deep within thick shrubs. Mates with same mate for several years. Prefers open fields with cattle or sheep, where it feeds on insects attracted to livestock. This is a western bird, reaching its eastern limit in the Oklahoma Panhandle.

in flight

juvenile

Black-crowned Night-Heron
Nycticorax nycticorax

SUMMER

Size: 22–27" (56–69 cm); up to 3½' wingspan

Male: A stocky, hunched and inactive heron with black back and crown, white belly, and gray wings. Long dark bill and bright-red eyes. Short dull-yellow legs. Breeding adult has 2 long white plumes on crown.

Female: same as male

Juvenile: golden-brown head and back with white spots, streaked breast, yellow-orange eyes, brown bill

Nest: platform; female and male build; 1 brood per year

Eggs: 3–5; light blue without markings

Incubation: 24–26 days; female and male incubate

Fledging: 42–48 days; female and male feed the young

Migration: complete migrator, to Texas and Mexico

Food: fish, aquatic insects

Compare: A perching Great Blue Heron (p. 253) looks twice the size of a Black-crowned. Look for a short-necked heron with a black back and crown.

Stan's Notes: A very secretive bird, this heron is most active near dawn and dusk (crepuscular). It hunts alone, but it nests in small colonies. Roosts in trees during the day. Often squawks if disturbed from the daytime roost. Often seen being harassed by other herons during days. Stalks quiet backwaters in search of small fish and crabs.

soaring

juvenile

soaring
juvenile

Bald Eagle
Haliaeetus leucocephalus

YEAR-ROUND
WINTER

Size: 31–37" (79–94 cm); up to 7½' wingspan

Male: White head and tail contrast sharply with the dark-brown-to-black body and wings. Large, curved yellow bill and yellow feet.

Female: same as male but larger

Juvenile: dark brown with white speckles and spots on the body and wings; gray bill

Nest: massive platform, usually in a tree; female and male build; 1 brood per year

Eggs: 2–3; off-white without markings

Incubation: 34–36 days; female and male incubate

Fledging: 75–90 days; female and male feed the young

Migration: partial to non-migrator, to southern states

Food: fish, carrion, birds (mainly ducks)

Compare: The Turkey Vulture (p. 43) lacks the white head and white tail of adult Bald Eagle. Turkey Vulture has two-toned wings and flies with its wings in a V shape, unlike the straight-out wing position of the Eagle.

Stan's Notes: Nearly became extinct due to DDT poisoning and illegal killing. Returns to the same nest each year, adding more sticks and enlarging it to huge proportions, at times up to 1,000 pounds (450 kg). In their midair mating ritual, one eagle flips upside down and locks talons with another. Both tumble, then break apart to continue flight. Not uncommon for juveniles to perform this mating ritual even though they have not reached breeding age. Long-term pair bond but will switch mates when not successful at reproducing. Juveniles attain the white head and tail at 4–5 years of age.

female
p. 103

male

Indigo Bunting
Passerina cyanea

Size: 5½" (14 cm)

Male: Vibrant-blue finch-like bird. Dark markings scattered on wings and tail.

Female: light-brown with faint markings

Juvenile: similar to female

Nest: cup; female builds; 2 broods per year

Eggs: 3–4; pale blue without markings

Incubation: 12–13 days; female incubates

Fledging: 10–11 days; female feeds the young

Migration: complete, to Mexico, Central America, and South America

Food: insects, seeds, fruit; will visit seed feeders

Compare: The male Eastern Bluebird (p. 77) and the male Blue Grosbeak (p. 75) are larger. Lacks the bluebird's rust-red chest and grosbeak's chestnut-colored wing bars and large bill.

Stan's Notes: Seen along woodland edges and in parks and yards, feeding on insects. Comes to seed feeders early in spring, before insects are plentiful. Usually only the males are noticed. The male often sings from treetops to attract a mate. The female is quiet. Actually a gray bird without blue pigment in its feathers, like Blue Jays and other blue birds, sunlight is refracted within the structure of the feathers, making them appear blue. Plumage is iridescent in direct sun, duller in shade. Molts in spring to acquire body feathers with gray tips, which quickly wear off, revealing the bright-blue plumage. Molts in fall and appears like the female during winter. Migrates at night in flocks of 5–10 birds. Males return before the females and juveniles, often to the nest site of the preceding year. Juveniles move to within a mile of their birth site.

female
p. 125

male

Blue Grosbeak

Passerina caerulea

SUMMER

Size: 7" (18 cm)

Male: Overall blue bird with 2 chestnut wing bars. Large gray-to-silver bill. Black around base of bill.

Female: overall brown with darker wings and tail, 2 tan wing bars, large gray-to-silver bill

Juvenile: similar to female

Nest: cup; female builds; 1–2 broods per year

Eggs: 3–6; pale blue without markings

Incubation: 11–12 days; female incubates

Fledging: 9–10 days; female and male feed the young

Migration: complete, to Central America, the Bahamas, Cuba, and Mexico

Food: insects, seeds; will come to seed feeders

Compare: The more common male Indigo Bunting (p. 73) is very similar, but it is smaller and lacks wing bars. The male Eastern Bluebird (p. 77) is the same size, but lacks the chestnut wing bars and oversized bill.

Stan's Notes: Found throughout Oklahoma. A bird of semi-open habitats such as overgrown fields, riversides, woodland edges, and fencerows. Visits seed feeders, where it is often confused with male Indigo Buntings. Frequently seen twitching and spreading its tail. The first-year males show only some blue, obtaining the full complement of blue feathers in the second winter. It has expanded northward, and its overall populations have increased over the past 30–40 years.

male

female

Eastern Bluebird
Sialia sialis

YEAR-ROUND

Size: 7" (18 cm)

Male: Sky-blue head, back, and tail. Rust-red breast and white belly.

Female: grayer than male, with a faint rusty breast and faint blue wings and tail

Juvenile: similar to female but with spots on the breast and blue wing markings

Nest: cavity, vacant woodpecker cavity or nest box; female adds a soft lining; 2 broods per year

Eggs: 4–5; pale blue without markings

Incubation: 12–14 days; female incubates

Fledging: 15–18 days; male and female feed the young

Migration: partial to non-migrator in Oklahoma

Food: insects, fruit; comes to shallow dishes with live or dead mealworms, and to suet feeders

Compare: Male Indigo Bunting (p. 73) is nearly all blue, lacking the rusty red breast. Blue Jay (p. 83) is considerably larger, with a crest and white markings.

Stan's Notes: A year-round resident throughout Oklahoma. Populations drop occasionally due to unseasonably cold winters or cold, wet weather in spring. Although it is a permanent resident, many migrate each spring and autumn. Prefers open habitats, such as farm fields, pastures, and roadsides, but also likes forest edges, parks, and yards. Easily tamed. Often perches on trees or fence posts and drops to the ground to grab bugs, especially grasshoppers. Makes short flights from tree to tree. Song is a distinctive "churlee chur chur-lee." The rust-red breast is like that of the American Robin, its cousin. Young of the first brood will help raise young of the second.

Barn Swallow
Hirundo rustica

SUMMER

Size: 7" (18 cm)

Male: Sleek swallow. Blue-black back, cinnamon belly, and reddish-brown chin. White spots on a long, deeply forked tail.

Female: same as male but with a whitish belly

Juvenile: similar to adults, with a tan belly and chin, and shorter tail

Nest: cup; female and male build; 2 broods per year

Eggs: 4–5; white with brown markings

Incubation: 13–17 days; female incubates

Fledging: 18–23 days; female and male feed the young

Migration: complete, to South America

Food: insects (prefers beetles, wasps, flies)

Compare: Cliff Swallow (p. 105) is smaller and lacks a distinctive, deeply forked tail. The Chimney Swift (p. 89) has a narrow pointed tail with wings longer than the body. Purple Martin (p. 81) is nearly 2 inches (5 cm) larger and has a dark-purple belly. Look for Barn Swallow's deeply forked tail.

Stan's Notes: Seen in wetlands, farms, suburban yards, and parks. Of the six swallow species regularly found in Oklahoma, this is the only one with a deeply forked tail. Unlike other swallows, it rarely glides in flight. Usually flies low over land or water. Drinks as it flies, skimming water, or will sip water droplets on wet leaves. Bathes while flying through rain or sprinklers. Gives a twittering warble, followed by a mechanical sound. Builds a mud nest with up to 1,000 beak-loads of mud. Nests on barns and houses, under bridges, and in other sheltered places. Often nests in colonies of 4–6 birds; sometimes nests alone.

male

female

Purple Martin
Progne subis

SUMMER MIGRATION

Size: 8½" (21.5 cm)

Male: Iridescent with a purple-to-black head, back, and belly. Black wings and a notched black tail.

Female: grayish-purple head and back, darker wings and tail, whitish belly

Juvenile: same as female

Nest: cavity; female and male line the cavity of the house; 1 brood per year

Eggs: 4–5; white without markings

Incubation: 15–18 days; female incubates

Fledging: 26–30 days; male and female feed the young

Migration: complete, to South America

Food: insects

Compare: Usually seen only in groups. The male Purple Martin is the only swallow with a very dark-purplish belly.

Stan's Notes: The largest swallow species in North America. Once nested in tree cavities in Oklahoma; now nests almost exclusively in man-made, apartment-style houses. The most successful colonies often nest in multiunit nest boxes within 100 feet (30 m) of a human dwelling near a lake. Main diet consists of dragonflies, not mosquitoes, as once thought. Gives a continuous stream of chirps, creaks and rattles, along with a shout-like "churrr" and chortle. Often drinks in flight, skimming water, and bathes in flight, flying through rain. Returns to the same nest site each year; the males arrive before the females and yearlings. The young leave to form new colonies. Large colonies gather in fall before migrating to South America.

Blue Jay
Cyanocitta cristata

Size: 12" (30 cm)

Male: Bright light-blue-and-white bird with a black necklace and gray belly. Large crest moves up and down at will. White face, wing bars, and tip of tail. Black tail bands.

Female: same as male

Juvenile: same as adult but duller

Nest: cup; female and male construct; 1–2 broods per year

Eggs: 4–5; green to blue with brown markings

Incubation: 16–18 days; female incubates

Fledging: 17–21 days; female and male feed the young

Migration: non-migrator to partial migrator; will move around to find an abundant food source

Food: insects, fruit, carrion, seeds, nuts; visits seed feeders, ground feeders with corn or peanuts

Compare: Eastern Bluebird (p. 77) is much smaller and lacks the crest. The Belted Kingfisher (p. 85) lacks the vivid blue coloring and black necklace of Blue Jay.

Stan's Notes: Highly intelligent, solving problems, gathering food, and communicating more than other birds. Loud and noisy; mimics other birds. Known as the alarm of the forest, screaming at intruders. Imitates hawk calls around feeders to scare off other birds. One of the few birds to cache food; can remember where it hid thousands of nuts. Carries food in a pouch under its tongue (sublingually). Eats eggs and young from other nests. Feathers lack blue pigment; refracted sunlight causes the blue appearance.

male

female

Belted Kingfisher
Megaceryle alcyon

YEAR-ROUND

Size: 12–14" (30–36 cm)

Male: Blue with white belly, blue-gray chest band, and black wing tips. Ragged crest moves up and down at will. Large head. Long, thick, black bill. White spot by eyes. Red-brown eyes.

Female: same as male but with rusty flanks and a rusty chest band below the blue-gray band

Juvenile: similar to female

Nest: cavity; female and male excavate in a bank of a river, lake or cliff; 1 brood per year

Eggs: 6–7; white without markings

Incubation: 23–24 days; female and male incubate

Fledging: 23–24 days; female and male feed the young

Migration: non-migrator in Oklahoma

Food: small fish

Compare: The Blue Jay (p. 83) is lighter blue and has a plain gray chest and belly. The Belted Kingfisher is rarely found away from water.

Stan's Notes: Usually found at the bank of a river, lake, or large stream. Perches on a branch near water, dives in headfirst to catch a small fish, then returns to the branch to feed. Parents drop dead fish into the water to teach their young to dive. Can't pass bones through its digestive tract; regurgitates bone pellets after meals. Loud call that sounds like a machine gun. Mates know each other by their calls. Digs a tunnel up to 4 feet (about 1 m) long to a nest chamber. Small white patches on dark wing tips flash during flight. Many northern birds move into the state in winter, increasing populations.

non-breeding

breeding

molting
juvenile

white
juvenile

SUMMER MIGRATION

Little Blue Heron
Egretta caerulea

Size: 22–26" (56–66 cm)

Male: Dark slate-blue to purple nearly all year. Dull-green legs and feet. Black-tipped blue-gray bill. Breeding adult has a reddish-purple head and neck with several long plumes on the crown.

Female: same as male

Juvenile: pure white overall, yellowish legs and feet, black-tipped gray bill

Nest: platform; female and male build; 1 brood per year

Eggs: 2–6; light blue without markings

Incubation: 20–23 days; female and male incubate

Fledging: 42–49 days; female and male feed the young

Migration: complete migrator, to coastal Texas, Mexico, Central and South America

Food: fish, aquatic insects

Compare: Snowy Egret (p. 289) can be confused with a juvenile Little Blue, but Snowy has bright-yellow feet, black legs and a solid black bill.

Stan's Notes: Unusual because the young look completely different from adults. All-white young turn blotchy white the first year. By the second year they look like the adult birds. A very slow stalker of prey in freshwater lakes and rivers, marshes, and wetlands. Nests in large colonies. Slowly expanding range in Oklahoma over the past decades.

87

Chimney Swift

Chaetura pelagica

SUMMER

Size: 5" (13 cm)

Male: Nondescript, cigar-shaped bird, usually seen in flight. Long, thin, brown body. Pointed tail and head. Long, backswept wings, longer than the body.

Female: same as male

Juvenile: same as adults

Nest: half cup; female and male construct; 1 brood per year

Eggs: 4–5; white without markings

Incubation: 19–21 days; female and male incubate

Fledging: 28–30 days; female and male feed the young

Migration: complete, to South America

Food: insects caught in midair

Compare: The Purple Martin (p. 81) is much larger and darker. The Barn Swallow (p. 79) has a deeply forked tail. Look for the cigar shape to identify the Chimney Swift in flight.

Stan's Notes: One of the fastest fliers in the bird world. Spends all day flying, rarely perching. Flies in groups, feeding on insects flying 100 feet (30 m) or higher up in the air. Often called a Flying Cigar due to its body shape, which is pointed at both ends. Drinks and bathes during flight, skimming water. Gives a unique in-flight twittering call, often heard before the bird is seen. Hundreds roost in large chimneys, giving it the common name. Builds its nest with tiny twigs, cementing it with saliva and attaching it to the inside of a chimney or a hollow tree. Usually only one nest per chimney.

Chipping Sparrow
Spizella passerina

SUMMER MIGRATION

Size:	5" (13 cm)
Male:	Small gray-brown sparrow with clear-gray chest. Rusty crown. White eyebrows and thin black eye line. Thin gray-black bill. Two faint wing bars.
Female:	same as male
Juvenile:	similar to adults, with streaking on the chest; lacks a rusty crown
Nest:	cup; female builds; 2 broods per year
Eggs:	3–5; blue-green with brown markings
Incubation:	11–14 days; female incubates
Fledging:	10–12 days; female and male feed the young
Migration:	complete to southern states, Mexico, and Central America
Food:	insects, seeds; will come to ground feeders
Compare:	Similar to American Tree Sparrow (p. 109), which shares a rusty crown but lacks dark eye line. The Lark Sparrow (p. 117) is larger and has a white chest and central spot. Song Sparrow (p. 107) and female House Finch (p. 95) have heavily streaked chests.

Stan's Notes: A common garden or yard bird, it is often seen feeding on dropped seeds beneath feeders. Gathers in large family groups to feed in preparation for migration. Migrates at night in flocks of 20–30 birds. The common name comes from the male's fast "chip" call. Often is just called Chippy. Builds nest low in dense shrubs and almost always lines it with animal hair. Comfortable with people, allowing you to approach closely before it flies away.

Pine Siskin
Spinus pinus

WINTER

Size: 5" (13 cm)

Male: Small brown finch with heavy streaking on the back, breast, and belly. Yellow wing bars. Yellow at the base of tail. Thin bill.

Female: similar to male, with less yellow

Juvenile: similar to adult, with a light-yellow tinge over the breast and chin

Nest: cup; female builds; 2 broods

Eggs: 3–4; greenish blue with brown markings

Incubation: 12–13 days; female incubates

Fledging: 14–15 days; female and male feed the young

Migration: irruptive; moves around the United States in search of food

Food: seeds, insects; will come to seed feeders

Compare: Female House Finch (p. 95) lacks any yellow. The female American Goldfinch (p. 299) has white wing bars. Female Purple Finch (p. 113) has bold white eyebrows. Look for the yellow wing bars to identify the Pine Siskin.

Stan's Notes: Usually considered a winter finch, seen in flocks of up to 20 birds, often with other finch species. While it can be found throughout Oklahoma in heavy invasion years, it is absent in many winters. Will come to thistle feeders. Gives a series of high-pitched, wheezy calls. Also gives a wheezing twitter. Breeds in small groups. Builds nest toward the end of coniferous branches, where needles are dense, helping to conceal. Nests are often only a few feet apart. Male feeds the female during incubation. Juveniles lose the yellow tint by late summer of their first year. Doesn't nest in Oklahoma.

male
p. 275

female

House Finch
Haemorhous mexicanus

YEAR-ROUND

Size: 5" (13 cm)

Female: Plain brown with heavy streaking on a white chest.

Male: red-to-orange face, throat, chest and rump, streaked belly and wings, brown cap, brown marking behind the eyes

Juvenile: similar to female

Nest: cup, occasionally in a cavity; female builds; 2 broods per year

Eggs: 4–5; pale blue, lightly marked

Incubation: 12–14 days; female incubates

Fledging: 15–19 days; female and male feed the young

Migration: non-migrator to partial migrator; moves around to find food

Food: seeds, fruit, leaf buds; visits seed feeders and feeders that offer grape jelly

Compare: The female Purple Finch (p. 113) is very similar but has bold white eyebrows. The female American Goldfinch (p. 299) has a clear chest and white wing bars. Similar to Pine Siskin (p. 93), but it lacks yellow wing bars and has a much larger bill than Siskin.

Stan's Notes: Can be a common bird at your feeders. A very social bird, visiting feeders in small flocks. Likes to nest in hanging flower baskets. Male sings a loud, cheerful warbling song. Historically, it occurred from the Pacific coast to the Rockies, with only a few reaching the eastern side. Now found throughout the country. Suffers from a disease that causes the eyes to crust, resulting in blindness and death.

Western

Eastern

Bewick's Wren
Thryomanes bewickii

YEAR-ROUND

Size: 5½" (14 cm)

Male: Brown cap, back, wings, and tail. Gray chest and belly. White chin and eyebrows. Long tail with white spots on edges is cocked and flits sideways. Pointed down-curved bill.

Female: same as male

Juvenile: similar to adult

Nest: cavity; female and male build nest in woodpecker hole or nest box; 2–3 broods a year

Eggs: 4–8; white with brown markings

Incubation: 12–14 days; female incubates

Fledging: 10–14 days; female and male feed young

Migration: non-migrator to partial

Food: insects, seeds

Compare: Similar to Carolina Wren (p. 99), but the Bewick's Wren has a gray chest.

Stan's Notes: A common wren of backyards and gardens. Insects make up 97 percent of its diet, with plant seeds composing the rest. Competes with Carolina Wrens for nesting cavities. Male will choose nesting cavities and start to build nests using small uniform-sized sticks. Female will make the final selection of a nest site and finish building. Begins breeding in April. Has 2–3 broods per year. Male feeds female while she incubates. Average size territory per pair is 5 acres (2 ha), which they defend all year long.

Carolina Wren
Thryothorus ludovicianus

YEAR-ROUND

Size: 5½" (14 cm)

Male: Rusty-brown head and back with an orange-yellow chest and belly. White throat and a prominent white eye stripe. Short, stubby tail, often cocked up.

Female: same as male

Juvenile: same as adults

Nest: cavity; female and male build; 2 broods per year, sometimes 3

Eggs: 4–6; white, sometimes pink or creamy, with brown markings

Incubation: 12–14 days; female incubates

Fledging: 12–14 days; female and male feed the young

Migration: non-migrator

Food: insects, fruit, few seeds; visits suet feeders

Compare: Bewick's Wren (p. 97) is similar but lacks Carolina Wren's orange-yellow chest and belly.

Stan's Notes: Mates are long-term, staying together throughout the year in permanent territories. Sings year-round. The male is known to sing up to 40 song types, singing one song repeatedly before switching to another. The female also sings, resulting in duets. The male often takes over feeding the first brood while the female renests. Nests in birdhouses and in unusual places like mailboxes, bumpers, or broken taillights of vehicles, or nearly any other cavity. Found in brushy yards or woodlands. Can be attracted to feeders with mealworms.

male
p. 215

female

Oregon
female

Dark-eyed Junco

Junco hyemalis

Size: 5½" (14 cm)

Female: A plump, dark-eyed bird with a tan-to-brown chest, head, and back. White belly. Ivory-to-pink bill. White outer tail feathers appear like a white V in flight.

Male: round bird with gray plumage

Juvenile: similar to female, with streaking on the breast and head

Nest: cup; female and male build; 2 broods per year

Eggs: 3–5; white with reddish-brown markings

Incubation: 12–13 days; female incubates

Fledging: 10–13 days; male and female feed the young

Migration: complete, throughout the U.S.; winters in Oklahoma

Food: seeds, insects; visits ground and seed feeders

Compare: Rarely confused with any other bird. Look for the ivory-to-pink bill and small flocks feeding beneath seed feeders to help identify the female Dark-eyed Junco.

Stan's Notes: Common in winter, this bird is usually seen on the ground in small flocks. Adheres to a rigid social hierarchy, with dominant birds chasing the less dominant birds. Look for the white outer tail feathers flashing in flight. Most comfortable on the ground, where it uses its feet to simultaneously "double-scratch" to expose seeds and insects. Eats many weed seeds. Several sub-species of Dark-eyed Junco were previously considered to be separate species but have now been combined into one. Doesn't nest in Oklahoma.

female

male
p. 73

Indigo Bunting
Passerina cyanea

SUMMER

Size: 5½" (14 cm)

Female: Light-brown, finch-like bird. Faint streaking on a light-tan chest. Wings have a very faint blue cast and indistinct wing bars.

Male: vibrant blue with scattered dark markings on wings and tail

Juvenile: similar to female

Nest: cup; female builds; 2 broods per year

Eggs: 3–4; pale blue without markings

Incubation: 12–13 days; female incubates

Fledging: 10–11 days; female feeds the young

Migration: complete, to Mexico, Central America, and South America

Food: insects, seeds, fruit; will visit seed feeders

Compare: Smaller than female Blue Grosbeak (p. 125) and lacking the grosbeak's tan wing bars. The female Purple Finch (p. 113) has white eyebrows and heavy streaking on the chest. The female House Finch (p. 95) has a heavily streaked chest. The female American Goldfinch (p. 299) has white wing bars.

Stan's Notes: Seen along woodland edges and in parks and yards, feeding on insects. Comes to seed feeders early in spring, before insects are plentiful. Secretive, plain, and quiet; usually only the males are noticed. The male often sings from treetops to attract a mate. Migrates at night in flocks of 5–10 birds. Males return before the females and juveniles, often to the nest site of the preceding year. Juveniles move to within a mile of their birth site.

Cliff Swallow
Petrochelidon pyrrhonota

Size: 5½" (14 cm)

Male: Uniquely patterned swallow with a dark back, wings, and cap. Distinctive tan-to-rust rump, cheeks, and forehead.

Female: same as male

Juvenile: similar to adult, lacks distinct patterning

Nest: gourd-shaped, made of mud; male and female build; 1–2 broods per year

Eggs: 4–6; pale white with brown markings

Incubation: 14–16 days; male and female incubate

Fledging: 21–24 days; female and male feed young

Migration: complete, to South America

Food: insects

Compare: Barn Swallow (p. 79) is larger and has a distinctive, deeply forked tail and blue back and wings.

Stan's Notes: A common and widespread swallow species in the state during the summer. Common around bridges (especially bridges over water) and rural housing (especially in open country near cliffs). Builds a gourd-shaped nest with a funnel-like entrance pointing down. A colony nester, with many nests lined up beneath building eaves or cliff overhangs. Will carry balls of mud up to a mile to construct its nest. Many in the colony return to the same nest site each year. Not unusual to have two broods per season. If the number of nests underneath eaves becomes a problem, wait until the young have left the nests to hose off the mud.

Song Sparrow
Melospiza melodia

WINTER

Size: 5–6" (13–15 cm)

Male: Common brown sparrow with heavy dark streaks on the chest coalescing into a central dark spot.

Female: same as male

Juvenile: similar to adults, with a finely streaked chest; lacks a central dark spot

Nest: cup; female builds; 2 broods per year

Eggs: 3–4; blue to green, with red-brown markings

Incubation: 12–14 days; female incubates

Fledging: 9–12 days; female and male feed the young

Migration: complete migrator, to southern states; winters in Oklahoma

Food: insects, seeds; only rarely comes to ground feeders with seeds

Compare: Similar to other brown sparrows. Look for the heavily streaked chest with a central dark spot to help identify the Song Sparrow.

Stan's Notes: There are many subspecies of this bird, but the dark spot in the center of the chest appears in every variety. A constant songster, repeating its loud, clear song every few minutes. The song varies from region to region but has the same basic structure. Sings from thick shrubs to defend a small territory, beginning with three notes and finishing up with a trill. A ground feeder, it will "double-scratch" with both feet at the same time to expose seeds. When the female builds a new nest for a second brood, the male often takes over feeding the first brood. Unlike many other sparrow species, Song Sparrows rarely flock together. A common host of the Brown-headed Cowbird.

American Tree Sparrow
Spizelloides arborea

WINTER

Size: 6" (15 cm)

Male: Brown with a tan chest and rusty crown and eye line. Gray eyebrows. Dark spot in the center of the chest. Dark upper bill; yellow lower bill. 2 white wing bars.

Female: same as male

Juvenile: streaked chest often obscures the central dark spot; lacks a rusty crown

Nest: cup; female builds; 1 brood per year

Eggs: 3–5; greenish white with brown markings

Incubation: 12–13 days; female incubates

Fledging: 8–10 days; female and male feed the young

Migration: complete, across North America; winters in Oklahoma

Food: insects, seeds; visits seed feeders

Compare: The Chipping Sparrow (p. 91) has white eyebrows and a black eye line. The Song Sparrow (p. 107) has a heavily streaked chest. To identify the American Tree Sparrow, check for the dark spot on the chest and the two-toned bill.

Stan's Notes: Commonly seen during spring and fall migrations in flocks of 2–200 birds. A regular winter bird feeder visitor in Oklahoma. Found in open fields, woodlands, and suburban back-yards. Sometimes called a Winter Chippy because it looks like the Chipping Sparrow, a summer visitor. Gives a series of high-pitched, sweet-sounding whistles. Nests in Canada and Alaska. The species name *arborea* means "tree," but it doesn't nest in trees; it nests on the ground in a clump of grass. The "Tree" in the name refers to its habitat. "American" refers to its natural range.

male

female

House Sparrow
Passer domesticus

YEAR-ROUND

Size: 6" (15 cm)

Male: Brown back with a gray belly and cap. Large black patch extending from the throat to the chest (bib). One white wing bar.

Female: slightly smaller than the male; light brown with light eyebrows; lacks a bib and white wing bar

Juvenile: similar to female

Nest: cavity; female and male build a domed cup nest within; 2–3 broods per year

Eggs: 4–6; white with brown markings

Incubation: 10–12 days; female incubates

Fledging: 14–17 days; female and male feed the young

Migration: non-migrator; moves around to find food

Food: seeds, insects, fruit; comes to seed feeders

Compare: American Tree Sparrow (p. 109) and Chipping Sparrow (p. 91) both have rusty-red crowns. Harris's Sparrow (p. 135) has a black "hood" and white chest. Look for the black bib to identify the male House Sparrow and the clear breast to help identify the female.

Stan's Notes: One of the first birdsongs heard in cities in spring. A familiar city bird, nearly always in small flocks. Also found on farms. Introduced in 1850 from Europe to Central Park in New York. Now seen throughout North America. Related to old-world sparrows; not a relative of any sparrows in the U.S. An aggressive bird that will kill young birds in order to take over the nest cavity. Uses dried grass and small scraps of plastic, paper, and other materials to build an oversized, domed nest in the cavity.

male
p. 277

female

Purple Finch
Haemorhous purpureus

WINTER

Size:	6" (15 cm)
Female:	plain brown with heavy streaking on the chest, bold white eyebrows and a large bill
Male:	raspberry-red head, cap, breast, back, and rump; brownish wings and tail
Juvenile:	same as female
Nest:	cup; female and male build; 1 brood per year
Eggs:	4–5; greenish blue with brown markings
Incubation:	12–13 days; female incubates
Fledging:	13–14 days; female and male feed the young
Migration:	irruptive; moves around in search of food
Food:	seeds, insects, fruit; comes to seed feeders
Compare:	The female House Finch (p. 95) lacks eyebrows. The Pine Siskin (p. 93) has yellow wing bars. The female American Goldfinch (p. 299) has a clear chest. Look for the bold white eyebrows to identify the female Purple Finch.

Stan's Notes: Usually only seen in the winter or during migration, when Purple Finches leave their northern homes and move around in search of food. Travels in flocks of up to 50 birds. Visits seed feeders along with House Finches, which makes it hard to tell them apart. Feeds mainly on seeds; ash tree seeds are an important source of food. Found in coniferous forests, mixed woods, woodland edges, and suburban backyards. Flies in the typical undulating, up-and-down pattern of finches. Sings a rich, loud song. Gives a distinctive "tic" note only in flight. The male is not purple. The Latin species name *purpureus* means "purple" (and other reddish colors).

male
p. 49

female

non-breeding
male

Lark Bunting
Calamospiza melanocorys

YEAR-ROUND
SUMMER

Size: 6½" (16 cm)

Female: Brown bird with heavily streaked chest and a white belly. Black vertical line on each side of white chin. May have a central dark spot on the chest. Faint white eyebrows.

Male: black bird with a large, broad head, white wing patches, and large bluish-gray bill

Juvenile: similar to adult of the same sex

Nest: cup; female builds; 1–2 broods per year

Eggs: 4–6; pale blue with markings

Incubation: 11–13 days; female and male incubate

Fledging: 8–12 days; female and male feed young

Migration: complete, to southwestern states; non-migrator in parts of Oklahoma

Food: insects, seeds

Compare: Appears similar to open-country sparrows. The female Red-winged Blackbird (p. 141) lacks the white belly and chin.

Stan's Notes: Common in western Oklahoma in dry plains and sagebrush regions. Has short, rounded wings. Flying with shallow wingbeats, the male flashes white wing patches. Male takes to air to display to female, setting its wings in a V position and floating back, rocking like a butterfly, singing a most amazing song. Song is like the song of Old World larks, hence the common name. Will flock with hundreds, if not thousands, of other Lark Buntings in autumn for migration.

Lark Sparrow
Chondestes grammacus

Size: 6½" (16 cm)

Male: All-brown bird with unique rust-red, white and black head pattern. A white breast with a central black spot. Gray rump and white edges to gray tail, as seen in flight.

Female: same as male

Juvenile: similar to adult, but no rust-red on head

Nest: cup, on the ground; female builds; 1 brood per year

Eggs: 3–6; pale white with brown markings

Incubation: 10–12 days; male and female incubate

Fledging: 10–12 days; female and male feed young

Migration: complete, to coastal Mexico, Central America

Food: seeds, insects

Compare: The White-throated Sparrow (p. 119) and White-crowned Sparrow (p. 121) both lack the Lark Sparrow's rust-red pattern on the head and central spot on a white chest. Larger than Chipping Sparrow (p. 91) has a similar rusty color on head, but it is smaller and lacks Lark Sparrow's white breast and central spot.

Stan's Notes: One of the larger sparrow species and one of the best songsters, also well known for its courtship strutting, chasing, and lark-like flight pattern (rapid wingbeats with tail spread). A bird of open fields, pastures, and prairies, found throughout the state but more abundant in the western half. Very common during migration, when large flocks congregate. Will use nest for several years if first brood is successful.

white-striped

tan-striped

White-throated Sparrow
Zonotrichia albicollis

MIGRATION WINTER

Size: 6–7" (15–18 cm)

Male: Brown with a gray or tan chest and belly. White or tan throat patch and eyebrows. Bold striping on the head. Small yellow spot in the space between the eye and bill, called the lore.

Female: same as male

Juvenile: similar to adults, with a heavily streaked chest and a gray throat and eyebrows

Nest: cup; female builds; 1 brood per year

Eggs: 4–6; green to blue, or cream-white with red-brown markings

Incubation: 11–14 days; female incubates

Fledging: 10–12 days; female and male feed the young

Migration: complete, to southern states and Mexico

Food: insects, seeds, fruit; visits ground feeders

Compare: White-crowned Sparrow (p. 121) lacks yellow lore and white or tan throat patch. The Lark Sparrow (p. 117) has a rust-red pattern on the head and central black spot on a white chest.

Stan's Notes: Two color variations (polymorphic): white-striped and tan-striped. Studies indicate that the white-striped adults tend to mate with the tan-striped birds; it's not clear why. Known for its wonderful song; it sings all year and can even be heard at night. White- and tan-striped males and white-striped females sing, but tan-striped females do not. No indication why. Seen during migration, often at ground feeders. Often associated with other sparrows in winter. Builds nest on the ground under small trees in bogs and coniferous forests. Doesn't nest in Oklahoma.

juvenile

White-crowned Sparrow
Zonotrichia leucophrys

Size: 6½–7½" (16.5–19 cm)

Male: Brown with a gray chest and black-and-white striped crown. Small, thin, pink bill.

Female: same as male

Juvenile: similar to adults, with black and brown stripes on the head

Nest: cup; female builds; 2 broods per year

Eggs: 3–5; greenish to bluish to whitish with red-brown markings

Incubation: 11–14 days; female incubates

Fledging: 8–12 days; male and female feed the young

Migration: complete, to southern states and Mexico; winters in Oklahoma

Food: insects, seeds, berries; visits ground feeders

Compare: The White-throated Sparrow (p. 119) has a white or tan throat patch, and yellow spot between the eyes and bill, with a blackish bill. Lark Sparrow (p. 117) has a rust-red pattern on the head and a central black spot on a white breast.

Stan's Notes: Often in groups of up to 20 birds during migrations, when it can be seen feeding underneath seed feeders. This ground feeder will "double-scratch" backward with both feet simultaneously to find seeds. The males are prolific songsters, singing in late winter while migrating north. Males take most of the responsibility for raising the young, while females start their second broods. Only 9–12 days separate the broods. Doesn't nest in Oklahoma.

Swainson's Thrush
Catharus ustulatus

MIGRATION

Size: 7" (18 cm)

Male: Dusty brown head, back, and wings. Brown smudges and spots, especially on its throat, chest, and off-white belly. A small, thin two-toned bill, yellow under and black above.

Female: same as male

Juvenile: overall lighter than adult, with less distinct spots on chest

Nest: cup; female builds; 1 brood per year

Eggs: 3–5; pale blue with brown markings

Incubation: 12–14 days; female incubates

Fledging: 10–14 days; female and male feed young

Migration: complete, to Mexico, Central America, and South America

Food: insects, fruit

Compare: Similar shape as American Robin (p. 231), but is smaller and lacks the red breast.

Stan's Notes: Seen during spring and fall migrations. Often is hard to see because most of the time it stays on the ground in thick vegetation. Song sounds like someone playing a flute. Feeds mostly on insects during spring and summer, adding fruit to its diet in late summer. Nests in shrubs or low in conifers, building a bulky nest consisting of grass, bark, and moss, all glued together with mud. Doesn't nest in Oklahoma.

male
p. 75

female

Blue Grosbeak
Passerina caerulea

Size: 7" (18 cm)

Female: Overall brown with darker wings and tail. Two tan wing bars. Large gray-to-silver bill.

Male: blue bird with 2 chestnut wing bars; large gray-to-silver bill; black around base of bill

Juvenile: similar to female

Nest: cup; female builds; 1–2 broods per year

Eggs: 3–6; pale blue without markings

Incubation: 11–12 days; female incubates

Fledging: 9–10 days; female and male feed the young

Migration: complete, to Central America, the Bahamas, Cuba, and Mexico

Food: insects, seeds; will come to seed feeders

Compare: The female Indigo Bunting (p. 103) is very similar, but it is smaller and more common than the female Blue Grosbeak. The female bunting lacks the Grosbeak's wing bars and large bill.

Stan's Notes: Found throughout Oklahoma. A bird of semi-open habitats such as overgrown fields, riversides, woodland edges, and fencerows. Visits seed feeders, where it can be confused with female Indigo Buntings. Often seen twitching and spreading its tail. The first-year males show only some blue, obtaining the full complement of blue feathers in the second winter. It has expanded northward, and its overall populations have increased over the past 30–40 years.

male
p. 51

female

Rose-breasted Grosbeak
Pheucticus ludovicianus

SUMMER MIGRATION

Size: 7–8" (18–20 cm)

Female: Plump and heavily streaked. Large, obvious white eyebrows. Large ivory bill. Orange-to-yellow wing linings.

Male: black and white with a triangular rose patch in the center of the chest, rose wing linings

Juvenile: similar to female

Nest: cup; female and male construct; 1–2 broods per year

Eggs: 3–5; blue-green with brown markings

Incubation: 13–14 days; female and male incubate

Fledging: 9–12 days; female and male feed the young

Migration: complete, to Mexico, Central America, and South America

Food: insects, seeds, fruit; comes to seed feeders

Compare: Looks like a large finch with bold white eyebrows and heavy streaking. The female Purple Finch (p. 113) has smaller eyebrows. The female House Finch (p. 95) lacks eyebrows.

Stan's Notes: Seen throughout Oklahoma during spring and fall migrations. Prefers a mature deciduous forest for nesting. Both sexes sing, but the male sings much louder and clearer. Sings a rich, robin-like song with a chip note in the tune. "Grosbeak" refers to the thick, strong bill, which is used to crush seeds. Males arrive at the breeding grounds a few days before females. Several males will visit seed feeders together in spring. When females arrive, males become territorial and reduce their feeder visits. After fledging, the young visit feeders with the adults. Makes short flights from tree to tree with rapid wingbeats. Doesn't nest in Oklahoma.

female

male

Horned Lark
Eremophila alpestris

Size: 7–8" (18–20 cm)

Male: Tan to brown with black markings on the face. Black necklace and bill. Pale-yellow chin. Two tiny feather "horns" on the top of the head, sometimes hard to see. Dark tail with white outer tail feathers, seen in flight.

Female: duller than male; less noticeable "horns"

Juvenile: lacks a yellow chin and black markings; does not develop "horns" until the second year

Nest: ground; female builds; 2–3 broods per year

Eggs: 3–4; gray with brown markings

Incubation: 11–12 days; female incubates

Fledging: 9–12 days; female and male feed the young

Migration: non-migrator to partial in Oklahoma

Food: seeds, insects

Compare: Western Meadowlark (p. 315) is larger and has a yellow breast and belly. Look for the black markings by the eyes and the black necklace to identify the Horned Lark.

Stan's Notes: The only true lark native to North America. A year-round resident, moving around in winter to find food. Larks are a bird of open ground. Common in rural areas; often seen in large flocks. The population increased in North America over the past century as more land was cleared for farming. Male performs a fluttering courtship flight high in the air while singing a high-pitched song. Female performs a fluttering distraction display when the nest is disturbed. Starts breeding early in the year. Able to renest about a week after the brood fledges. Moves around in winter to find food. "Lark" comes from the Middle English *laverock*, or "a lark."

male
p. 25

female

Brown-headed Cowbird
Molothrus ater

Size: 7½" (19 cm)

Female: Dull brown with no obvious markings. Pointed, sharp, gray bill. Dark eyes.

Male: glossy black with a chocolate-brown head

Juvenile: similar to female but with dull-gray plumage and a streaked chest

Nest: no nest; lays eggs in the nests of other birds

Eggs: 5–7; white with brown markings

Incubation: 10–13 days; host birds incubate the eggs

Fledging: 10–11 days; host birds feed the young

Migration: non-migrator in Oklahoma

Food: insects, seeds; will come to seed feeders

Compare: The female Red-winged Blackbird (p. 141) has white eyebrows and heavy streaking. European Starling (p. 27) has speckles and a shorter tail. The pointed gray bill helps to identify the female Brown-headed Cowbird.

Stan's Notes: Cowbirds are members of the blackbird family. Of approximately 750 species of parasitic birds worldwide, this is the only parasitic bird in Oklahoma. Brood parasites lay their eggs in the nests of other birds, leaving the host birds to raise their young. Cowbirds are known to have laid their eggs in the nests of over 200 species of birds. While some birds reject cowbird eggs, most incubate them and raise the young, even to the exclusion of their own. Look for warblers and other birds feeding young birds twice their own size. Named "Cowbird" for its habit of following bison and cattle herds to feed on insects flushed up by the animals.

juvenile

Bohemian
Waxwing

Cedar Waxwing
Bombycilla cedrorum

WINTER

Size: 7½" (19 cm)

Male: Sleek-looking, gray-to-brown bird. Pointed crest, bandit-like mask, and light-yellow belly. Bold-yellow tip of tail. Red wing tips look like they were dipped in red wax.

Female: same as male

Juvenile: grayish with a heavily streaked breast; lacks the sleek look, black mask, and red wing tips

Nest: cup; female and male construct; 1 brood per year, occasionally 2

Eggs: 4–6; pale blue with brown markings

Incubation: 10–12 days; female incubates

Fledging: 14–18 days; female and male feed the young

Migration: partial migrator; moves around to find food

Food: cedar cones, fruit, insects

Compare: Similar to its larger, less common cousin, Bohemian Waxwing (see inset). Look for the red wing tips, yellow-tipped tail, and black mask to identify the Cedar Waxwing.

Stan's Notes: The name is derived from its red, wax-like wing tips, and preference for the small, berry-like cones of the cedar. Seen in flocks, moving around from area to area, looking for berries. Feeds on insects during summer, before berries are abundant. Wanders during winter, searching for food supplies. Spends most of its time at the top of tall trees. Listen for the high-pitched "sreee" whistling sound it constantly makes while perched or in flight. Obtains the mask after the first year and red wing tips after the second year.

juvenile

Harris's Sparrow
Zonotrichia querula

WINTER

Size: 7½" (19 cm)

Male: A very large sparrow with various amounts of black on head, extending down the nape and face onto the chest. White belly. Brown back and wings. Pink bill and legs.

Female: same as male

Juvenile: similar to adult, lacks the black "hood" and spotted chest

Nest: cup, on the ground; unknown who builds; 1 brood per year

Eggs: 4–5; white with brown markings

Incubation: 13–14 days; female incubates

Fledging: 11–12 days; female and male feed young

Migration: complete, to southern states; winters in Oklahoma

Food: insects, seeds, berries, ground feeders

Compare: House Sparrow (p. 111) lacks the Harris's black "hood."

Stan's Notes: A large sparrow commonly seen in small groups of up to ten birds scratching under seed feeders during spring and fall migrations. Nests in northern Canada, returning to Oklahoma and the central U.S. for winter. Recent studies show that a bird's status is dependent upon the amount of black on its "hood," not its age. The more black, the higher the status. Named after Edward Harris (1799–1863), a companion of John James Audubon.

winter

breeding

Spotted Sandpiper

Actitis macularius

SUMMER MIGRATION

Size: 8" (20 cm)

Male: Olive-brown back with black spots on a white chest and belly. White line over eyes. Long, dull-yellow legs. Long bill. Winter plumage lacks spots on the chest and belly.

Female: same as male

Juvenile: similar to winter plumage, with a darker bill

Nest: ground; male builds; 2 broods per year

Eggs: 3–4; brownish with brown markings

Incubation: 20–24 days; male incubates

Fledging: 17–21 days; male feeds the young

Migration: complete migrator, to southern states, Mexico, Central and South America

Food: aquatic insects

Compare: Lesser Yellowlegs (p. 155) is larger. Killdeer (p. 157) has 2 black neck bands. Look for the black spots on the chest and belly and the bobbing tail to help identify the breeding Spotted Sandpiper.

Stan's Notes: One of the few shorebirds that will dive underwater when pursued. Able to fly straight up out of the water. Holds wings in a cup-like arc in flight, rarely lifting them above a horizontal plane. Walks as if delicately balanced. When standing, constantly bobs its tail. Gives a rapid series of "weet-weet-weet" calls when frightened and flying away. Female mates with multiple males and lays eggs in up to five nests. Male does all of the nest building, incubating, and childcare without any help from the female.

male
p. 281

female

juvenile

Northern Cardinal
Cardinalis cardinalis

Size: 8–9" (20–23 cm)

Female: Buff-brown with red tinges on the crest and wings. Black mask and a large reddish bill.

Male: red with a large crest and bill and a black mask extending from the face to the throat

Juvenile: same as female but with a blackish-gray bill

Nest: cup; female builds; 2–3 broods per year

Eggs: 3–4; bluish white with brown markings

Incubation: 12–13 days; female and male incubate

Fledging: 9–10 days; female and male feed the young

Migration: non-migrator

Food: seeds, insects, fruit; comes to seed feeders

Compare: The Cedar Waxwing (p. 133) has a small dark bill. The juvenile Northern Cardinal (bottom inset) looks like the adult female but with a dark bill. Look for the reddish bill to identify the female Northern Cardinal.

Stan's Notes: A familiar backyard bird. Seen in a variety of habitats, including parks. Usually likes thick vegetation. One of the few species in which both females and males sing. Can be heard all year. Listen for its "whata-cheer-cheer-cheer" territorial call in spring. Watch for a male feeding a female during courtship. The male also feeds the young of the first brood while the female builds a second nest. Territorial in spring, fighting its own reflection in a window or other reflective surface. Non-territorial in winter, gathering in small flocks of up to 20 birds. *Cardinalis* denotes importance, as represented by the red priestly garments of Catholic cardinals.

male
p. 31

female

Red-winged Blackbird
Agelaius phoeniceus

YEAR-ROUND

Size: 8½" (22 cm)

Female: Heavily streaked brown body. Pointed brown bill and white eyebrows.

Male: jet black with red-and-yellow shoulder patches (epaulets) and a pointed black bill

Juvenile: same as female

Nest: cup; female builds; 2–3 broods per year

Eggs: 3–4; bluish green with brown markings

Incubation: 10–12 days; female incubates

Fledging: 11–14 days; female and male feed the young

Migration: non-migrator to partial migrator

Food: seeds, insects; visits seed and suet feeders

Compare: Female Yellow-headed Blackbird (p. 151) is larger. Female Brown-headed Cowbird (p. 131) is smaller. Both species lack white eyebrows and heavily streaked chest of the female Red-winged Blackbird. Thinner body than female Rose-breasted Grosbeak (p. 127) and has a pointed bill.

Stan's Notes: One of the most widespread and numerous birds in Oklahoma. Found around marshes, wetlands, lakes, and rivers. Flocks with as many as 10,000 birds have been reported. Males arrive before females and sing to defend their territory. The male repeats his call from the top of a cattail while showing off his red-and-yellow shoulder patches. The female chooses a mate and often builds her nest over shallow water in a thick stand of cattails. The male can be aggressive when defending the nest. Feeds mostly on seeds in spring and fall and insects throughout the summer.

141

male
p. 29

female

Eastern
Towhee

Spotted Towhee
Pipilo maculatus

WINTER

Size: 8½" (22 cm)

Female: A brown head, dirty red-brown sides and a white belly. Multiple white spots on wings and sides. Long black tail with white tip. Rich red eyes.

Male: mostly black, lacking the brown head

Juvenile: brown with a heavily streaked chest

Nest: cup; female builds; 1–2 broods per year

Eggs: 3–5; white with brown markings

Incubation: 12–14 days; female and male incubate

Fledging: 10–12 days; female and male feed young

Migration: complete migrator; winters in Oklahoma

Food: seeds, fruit, insects

Compare: American Robin (p. 231) is larger. Female Rose-breasted Grosbeak (p. 127) has a streaked breast and white eyebrows.

Stan's Notes: Once considered a single species, Spotted Towhee and Eastern Towhee were known as Rufous-sided Towhee. Spotted Towhees are seen throughout Oklahoma, while Eastern Towhees are found in the eastern part of the state. Found in a variety of habitats from thick brush and forest edges to suburban back-yards. Usually heard noisily scratching through dead leaves on the ground for food. Over 70 percent of its diet is plant material. Eats more insects during spring and summer. Well known to retreat from danger by walking away rather than taking flight. Nest is nearly always on the ground under bushes but away from where the male perches to sing. Song and plumage vary geographically and aren't well studied or understood.

female

male

Common Nighthawk

Chordeiles minor

SUMMER

Size: 9" (23 cm)

Male: Camouflaged brown and white with a white chin. Distinctive white band across the wings and tail, seen only in flight.

Female: similar to male, with a tan chin; lacks a white tail band

Juvenile: similar to female

Nest: no nest; lays eggs on the ground, usually on rocks, or on rooftop; 1 brood per year

Eggs: 2; cream with lavender markings

Incubation: 19–20 days; female and male incubate

Fledging: 20–21 days; female and male feed the young

Migration: complete, to South America

Food: insects caught in the air

Compare: Chimney Swift (p. 89) is much smaller. Look for the white chin, obvious white band on the wings and characteristic flap-flap-flap-glide pattern to help identify the Common Nighthawk.

Stan's Notes: Usually only seen in flight at dusk or after sunset but not uncommon to see it sleeping on a branch during the day. A prolific insect eater and very noisy in flight, repeating a "peenting" call. Alternates slow wingbeats with bursts of quick wingbeats. In cities, prefers to nest on flat rooftops with gravel. City populations are on the decline as gravel rooftops are converted to other styles. In spring, the male performs a showy mating ritual consisting of a steep diving flight ending with a loud popping noise. One of the first birds to migrate in fall, starting in August. Often seen in large flocks.

Burrowing Owl
Athene cunicularia

YEAR-ROUND
SUMMER

Size: 9–10" (24 cm); up to 2' wingspan

Male: A brown owl with bold white spots and a white belly. Yellow eyes and very long legs.

Female: same as male

Juvenile: same as adult, but belly is brown

Nest: cavity, former underground mammal den; female and male line den; 1 brood per year

Eggs: 6–11; white without markings

Incubation: 26–30 days; female incubates

Fledging: 25–28 days; female and male feed young

Migration: complete, to Mexico and Central America; winters in western Oklahoma

Food: insects, mammals, lizards, birds

Compare: Great Horned Owl (p. 197) is more than twice the size of Burrowing Owl and has feather tuft "horns." Burrowing spends most of its time on the ground, unlike tree-loving Great Horned.

Stan's Notes: An owl of fields, open backyards, golf courses, and airports. Nests in large family units or in small colonies. Takes over the underground dens of mammals, occasionally widening its den by kicking dirt backward. Lines den with cow pies, horse dung, grass, and feathers. Some people have had success attracting these owls to their backyards by creating artificial dens. Often seen during the day, standing or sleeping around den entrance. Male brings food to incubating female, often moving family to a new den when young are just a few weeks old. Will bob head up and down while doing deep knee bends when agitated or threatened.

in flight

juvenile

male

female

in-flight
juvenile

American Kestrel
Falco sparverius

Size: 9–11" (23–28 cm); up to 2' wingspan

Male: Rust-brown back and tail. White breast with dark spots. Two vertical black lines on a white face. Blue-gray wings. Wide black band with a white edge on the tip of a rusty tail.

Female: similar to male but slightly larger, with rust-brown wings and dark bands on the tail

Juvenile: same as adult of the same sex

Nest: cavity; does not build a nest; 1 brood per year

Eggs: 4–5; white with brown markings

Incubation: 29–31 days; male and female incubate

Fledging: 30–31 days; female and male feed the young

Migration: non-migrator to partial migrator; moves around in winter

Food: insects, small mammals and birds, reptiles

Compare: The Peregrine Falcon (p. 245) is much larger and has a dark "hood" marking. No other small bird of prey has a rusty back and tail.

Stan's Notes: An unusual raptor because the sexes look different (dimorphic). Due to its small size, this falcon was once called a Sparrow Hawk. Hovers near roads, then dives for prey. Watch for it to pump its tail after landing on a perch. Perches nearly upright. Eats many grasshoppers. Adapts quickly to a wooden nest box. Can be extremely vocal, giving a loud series of high-pitched calls. Ability to see ultraviolet (UV) light helps it locate mice and other prey by their urine, which glows bright yellow in UV light.

male
p. 33

female

Yellow-headed Blackbird

Xanthocephalus xanthocephalus

SUMMER MIGRATION

Size: 9–11" (23–28 cm)

Female: Large brown bird with a dull-yellow head and chest. Slightly smaller than the male.

Male: black bird with a lemon-yellow head, breast and nape of neck, black mask, gray bill, and white wing patches

Juvenile: similar to female

Nest: cup; female builds; 2 broods per year

Eggs: 3–5; greenish white with brown markings

Incubation: 11–13 days; female incubates

Fledging: 9–12 days; female feeds the young

Migration: complete, to southern states and Mexico

Food: insects, seeds; will come to ground feeders

Compare: Female Red-winged Blackbird (p. 141) is smaller and has white eyebrows and heavy streaking. Look for the dull-yellow head to help identify the female Yellow-headed.

Stan's Notes: Found around marshes, wetlands, and lakes. Nests in deep water, unlike its cousin, the Red-winged Blackbird, which prefers shallow water. Usually heard before seen. Gives a raspy, low, metallic-sounding call. The male is the only large black bird with a bright-yellow head. He gives an impressive mating display, flying with his head drooped and feet and tail pointing down while steadily beating his wings. Young keep low and out of sight for up to three weeks before they start to fly. Migrates in large flocks of as many as 200 birds, often with Red-winged Blackbirds and Brown-headed Cowbirds. Flocks of mainly males return in late March and early April; females return later. Most colonies consist of 20–100 nests.

male

female

Northern Bobwhite
Colinus virginianus

Size: 10" (25 cm)

Male: Short, stocky, and mostly brown with short gray tail. Prominent white eye stripe and white chin. Reddish-brown sides and belly, often with black lines and dots.

Female: similar to male, with buff-brown eye stripe and chin

Juvenile: smaller and duller than adults

Nest: ground; female and male construct; 1 brood per year

Eggs: 12–15; white to creamy without markings

Incubation: 23–24 days; female and male incubate

Fledging: 6–7 days; female and male feed the young

Migration: non-migrator

Food: insects, seeds, fruit; will come to ground feeders offering corn and millet

Compare: Ring-necked Pheasant (p. 201) is larger and has a long tail. Male pheasant is more colorful, and the female lacks a white chin.

Stan's Notes: Prefers shrubs, orchards, hedgerows, and pastures. Moves around in small flocks of 20 birds (often family members), called a covey. The covey often rests together during the night, in a tight circle with tails together and heads facing outward, to watch for predators. Males and females perform distraction displays when nests or young are threatened. Nest is a depression in the ground lined with grass. Often pulls nearby vegetation over nest to help conceal it. Male gives a rising whistle, "bob-white," heard mainly in spring and summer. Also gives a single "hoy" call year-round.

Lesser Yellowlegs
Tringa flavipes

Size: 10–12" (25–30 cm)

Male: A typical sandpiper-type bird with a brown back and wings. Streaked white chest. Thin, straight black bill. Long yellow legs.

Female: same as male

Juvenile: same as adults

Nest: ground; female builds; 1 brood per year

Eggs: 3–4; yellowish with brown markings

Incubation: 22–23 days; male and female incubate

Fledging: 18–20 days; male and female lead the young to food

Migration: complete, to South America

Food: aquatic insects, tiny fish

Compare: The breeding Spotted Sandpiper (p. 137) has black spots on its chest. Look for the straight black bill and long yellow legs of Lesser Yellowlegs.

Stan's Notes: Usually seen in large flocks, combing shorelines and mudflats in search of aquatic insects. Usually walks with its head down and tail up, ready to snatch up prey. Uses its long, straight bill to pluck insects and tiny fish out of the water. A member of the sandpiper group known as Tattlers, which scream alarm calls when taking off. Quite often moves into the water before taking flight and gives a variety of flight notes at takeoff. Nest is a simple depression atop a mound of earth. Nests in marshes in the spruce forests of central Alaska and Canada. The nest is a simple depression atop a mound of earth.

Killdeer
Charadrius vociferus

Size: 11" (28 cm)

Male: Upland shorebird with 2 black bands around the neck, like a necklace. Brown back and white belly. Bright reddish-orange rump, visible in flight.

Female: same as male

Juvenile: similar to adults, with a single neck band

Nest: ground; male scrapes; 2 broods per year

Eggs: 3–5; tan with brown markings

Incubation: 24–28 days; male and female incubate

Fledging: 25 days; male and female lead their young to food

Migration: complete, to southern states, Mexico, and Central America; non-migrator in Oklahoma

Food: insects, worms, snails

Compare: The Spotted Sandpiper (p. 137) is found around water but lacks the 2 neck bands of the Killdeer.

Stan's Notes: Technically classified as a shorebird but lives in dry habitats instead of the shore. Often found in vacant fields, gravel pits, driveways, wetland edges, or along railroad tracks. The only shorebird that has two black neck bands. Known to fake a broken wing to draw intruders away from the nest; once the nest is safe, the parent will take flight. Nests are just a slight depression in a dry area and are often hard to see. Hatchlings look like miniature adults walking on stilts. Soon after hatching, the young follow their parents around and peck for insects. Gives a loud and distinctive "kill-deer" call. Migrates in small flocks.

Brown Thrasher

Toxostoma rufum

YEAR-ROUND
SUMMER

Size: 11" (28 cm)

Male: Rust-red with a long tail. Heavy streaking on the breast and belly. Two white wing bars. Long, curved bill and bright-yellow eyes.

Female: same as male

Juvenile: same as adults but with grayish eyes

Nest: cup; female and male build; 2 broods per year

Eggs: 4–5; pale blue with brown markings

Incubation: 11–14 days; female and male incubate

Fledging: 10–13 days; female and male feed the young

Migration: complete, to southern states; non-migrator in most of Oklahoma

Food: insects, fruit

Compare: American Robin (p. 231) and Gray Catbird (p. 227) are similar, but both are smaller and lack a streaked chest, rusty color, and yellow eyes. Look for the long rusty-red tail to help identify the Brown Thrasher.

Stan's Notes: A prodigious songster. Sings along forest edges and in suburban yards. Often found in thick shrubs, where it will sing deliberate musical phrases, repeating each twice. The male Brown Thrasher has the largest documented repertoire of all North American songbirds, with more than 1,100 types of songs. Builds nest low in dense shrubs, often in fencerows. Quickly flies or runs on the ground in and out of thick shrubs. A noisy feeder due to its habit of turning over leaves, small rocks, and branches to find food. This bird is more abundant in the central Great Plains than anywhere else in North America.

yellow-shafted
male

yellow-shafted
female

red-shafted
male

red-shafted
female

Northern Flicker
Colaptes auratus

YEAR-ROUND

Size: 12" (30 cm)

Male: Brown and black with a red or black mustache and black necklace. Speckled chest. Large white rump patch, seen only when flying.

Female: same as male but without a mustache

Juvenile: same as adult of the same sex

Nest: cavity; female and male excavate; 1 brood per year

Eggs: 5–8; white without markings

Incubation: 11–14 days; female and male incubate

Fledging: 25–28 days; female and male feed the young

Migration: non-migrator in Oklahoma; moves around to find food

Food: insects (especially ants and beetles); comes to suet feeders

Compare: Male Red-bellied Woodpecker (p. 57) has a black-and-white zebra-striped back, red cap, and lacks a mustache. Flickers are the only brown-backed woodpeckers in Oklahoma.

Stan's Notes: This is the only woodpecker to regularly feed on the ground. Prefers ants and beetles and produces an antacid saliva that neutralizes the acidic defense of ants. Flickers in Oklahoma have golden yellow wing linings and tails. The red-shafted variety visits in winter. Male yellow-shafteds have black mustaches; male red-shafteds have red mustaches. Often reuses an old nest. Undulates deeply during flight, flashing color under its wings and tail and calling "wacka-wacka" loudly. Hybrids between yellow- and red-shafteds occur in the Great Plains where ranges overlap. Only the yellow-shafteds breed in Oklahoma.

Yellow-billed Cuckoo
Coccyzus americanus

Size: 12" (30 cm)

Male: Grayish brown head, back, wings, and tail. White chin, chest, and belly. Undertail distinctively patterned with bold black-and-white spots and lines. Long downward-curved bill. Lower bill (mandible) is yellow.

Female: same as male

Juvenile: similar to adult, but undertail lacks bold black-and-white pattern, and bill lacks yellow

Nest: platform; female and male construct; 1–2 broods per year

Eggs: 2–6; light blue without markings

Incubation: 9–11 days; female and male incubate

Fledging: 7–9 days; female and male feed the young

Migration: complete, to South America

Food: insects

Compare: The large-size, curved bill, and bold black-and-white undertail markings make this bird hard to confuse with others.

Stan's Notes: Common summer resident throughout the state. Found in a wide variety of habitats, but usually nests along forest edges. Often will place a flimsy stick nest in a densely covered tree fork. Unlike many other birds, the young do not hatch at the same time (asynchronously). There can be many days between the first and last to hatch. A very short egg-to-fledging time with some young leaving the nest (fledging) after only one week. The first to fledge are attended by the male, while the female cares for the rest in the nest. Declining in population in many states.

Mourning Dove
Zenaida macroura

Size: 12" (30 cm)

Male: Smooth and fawn-colored. Gray patch on the head. Iridescent pink and greenish blue on the neck. Black spot behind and below the eyes. Black spots on the wings and tail. Pointed, wedged tail; white edges seen in flight.

Female: similar to male, but lacks the pink-and-green iridescent neck feathers

Juvenile: spotted and streaked plumage

Nest: platform; female and male build; 2 broods per year

Eggs: 2; white without markings

Incubation: 13–14 days; male incubates during the day, female incubates at night

Fledging: 12–14 days; female and male feed the young

Migration: non-migrator to partial migrator; will move around to find food

Food: seeds; will visit seed and ground feeders

Compare: Eurasian Collared-Dove (p. 235) has a black collar on the nape of its neck. Rock Pigeon (p. 237) is larger and has a wide range of color combinations.

Stan's Notes: Name comes from its mournful cooing. A ground feeder, bobbing its head as it walks. One of the few birds to drink without lifting its head, like the Rock Pigeon (p. 237). The parents feed the young (squab) a regurgitated liquid called crop-milk for their first few days of life. Platform nest is flimsy and often falls apart in storms. During takeoff and in flight, wind rushes through the bird's wing feathers, creating a characteristic whistling sound.

Upland Sandpiper
Bartramia longicauda

Size: 12" (30 cm)

Male: Overall brown shorebird. Long yellow legs, a short, brown-tipped yellow bill, and white belly. Appears to have a thin neck and small head in relationship to its body.

Female: same as male

Juvenile: similar to adult

Nest: ground; female and male construct; 1 brood per year

Eggs: 3–4; off-white with red markings

Incubation: 21–27 days; female and male incubate

Fledging: 30–31 days; female and male feed young

Migration: complete, to South America

Food: insects, seeds

Compare: Breeding Spotted Sandpiper (p. 137) is smaller, has shorter legs, black spots on a white breast and is found in very different habitats. The Spotted Sandpiper is almost always near water while the Upland is in grassy meadows and prairies.

Stan's Notes: A shorebird of the dry grassland that is aptly named. Often seen standing on fence posts or other perches in a prairie or grassland habitat. Frequently found in prairies and grasslands that were burned, where foraging for food is easier. A true indicator of high-quality prairie habitat, this shorebird returns to a more watery habitat after breeding and just before migrating. Frequently holds its wings open over its back for several seconds just after landing. Formerly known as Upland Plover. Was hunted in the late 1800s.

167

male
p. 39

female

Great-tailed Grackle
Quiscalus mexicanus

YEAR-ROUND

Size: 15" (38 cm), female
18" (45 cm), male

Female: An overall brown bird with a gray-to-brown belly. Light-brown-to-white eyes, eyebrows, throat, and upper portion of chest.

Male: all-black bird with iridescent purple sheen on the head and back, exceptionally long tail, bright-yellow eyes

Juvenile: similar to female

Nest: cup; female builds; 1–2 broods per year

Eggs: 3–5; greenish blue with brown markings

Incubation: 12–14 days; female incubates

Fledging: 21–23 days; female feeds the young

Migration: non-migrator to partial migrator; moves around to find food

Food: insects, fruit, seeds; comes to seed feeders

Compare: The female Brown-headed Cowbird (p. 131) is much smaller than the Great-tailed female.

Stan's Notes: This is our largest grackle. It was once considered a subspecies of the Boat-tailed Grackle, which occurs along the East Coast and Florida. Prefers to nest close to water in an open habitat. A colony nester. Males do not participate in nest building, incubation, or raising young. Males rarely fight; females squabble over nest sites and materials. Several females mate with one male. The species is expanding northward, moving into northern states. Western populations tend to be larger than eastern. Song varies from population to population.

male

female

Green-winged Teal
Anas crecca

Size: 14–15" (36–38 cm)

Male: Chestnut head with a dark-green patch outlined with white from the eyes to the nape of neck. Gray body and butter-yellow tail. Green patch on the wings (speculum), seen in flight.

Female: light-brown duck with black spots and a green speculum, small bill

Juvenile: same as female

Nest: ground; female builds; 1 brood per year

Eggs: 8–10; cream-white without markings

Incubation: 21–23 days; female incubates

Fledging: 32–34 days; female teaches the young to feed

Migration: complete, to southern states; winters in Oklahoma

Food: aquatic plants and insects

Compare: The male Wood Duck (p. 263) is more colorful than the male Green-winged. Female Blue-winged Teal (p. 173) is similar in size, but it is slightly white at the base of its bill.

Stan's Notes: A common winter duck in the state. It is one of the smallest dabbling ducks, tipping forward in water to glean aquatic plants and insects from the bottom of shallow ponds. This behavior makes it vulnerable to ingesting spent lead shot, which can cause death. It walks well on land and will also feed in flooded fields and woodlands. Known for its fast and agile flight. Groups wheel and spin through the air in tight formation. The green wing patches are most obvious during flight.

male

female

Blue-winged Teal
Spatula discors

SUMMER

Size: 15–16" (38–41 cm)

Male: Small, plain-looking brown duck with black speckles and a large, crescent-shaped white mark at the base of the bill. Gray head. Black tail with a small white patch. Blue wing patch (speculum), best seen in flight.

Female: duller than male, with only slight white at the base of the bill; lacks a crescent mark on the face and a white patch on the tail

Juvenile: same as female

Nest: ground; female builds; 1 brood per year

Eggs: 8–11; creamy white

Incubation: 23–27 days; female incubates

Fledging: 35–44 days; female feeds the young

Migration: complete, to southern states, Mexico, and Central America

Food: aquatic plants, seeds, aquatic insects

Compare: The female Mallard (p. 185) has an orange-and-black bill. The female Wood Duck (p. 177) has a crest. Female Green-winged Teal (p. 171) is similar in size but lacks white at base of bill. Look for the white facial mark to identify the male Blue-winged.

Stan's Notes: One of the few breeding ducks in Oklahoma. Most breeding birds here leave before more-northern ducks pass through in autumn. Constructs nest some distance from water. Female performs a distraction display to protect nest and young. Male leaves female near the end of incubation. Planting crops and cultivating to pond edges have caused a decline in population.

male p. 61

female

Lesser Scaup
Aythya affinis

WINTER

Size: 16–17" (40–43 cm)

Female: Overall brown duck with a dull-white patch at the base of a light-gray bill. Yellow eyes.

Male: white and gray; the chest and head appear nearly black but the head looks purple with green highlights in direct sun; yellow eyes

Juvenile: same as female

Nest: ground; female builds; 1 brood per year

Eggs: 8–14; olive-buff without markings

Incubation: 22–28 days; female incubates

Fledging: 45–50 days; female teaches young to feed

Migration: complete, to southern states, Mexico, Central America, and northern South America

Food: aquatic plants and insects

Compare: The male Blue-winged Teal (p. 173) is slightly smaller and has a crescent-shaped white mark at the base of its bill. The female Wood Duck (p. 177) is larger with white around the eyes. Look for the white patch at the base of the bill to help identify the female Lesser Scaup.

Stan's Notes: A common wintering duck in the state, often seen in large flocks on lakes, ponds, and sewage lagoons. Submerges itself completely to feed on the bottom of lakes (unlike dabbling ducks, which only tip forward to reach the bottom). Note the bold white stripe under the wings when in flight. The male leaves the female when she starts incubating eggs. The quantity of eggs (clutch size) increases with the age of the female. This species has an interesting babysitting arrangement in which groups of young (crèches) are tended by one to three adult females.

male
p. 263

female

Wood Duck
Aix sponsa

Size: 17–20" (43–51 cm)

Female: Small brown dabbling duck. Bright-white eye-ring and a not-so-obvious crest. Blue patch on wings (speculum), often hidden.

Male: highly ornamented, with a mostly green head and crest patterned with black and white; rusty chest, white belly, and red eyes

Juvenile: similar to female

Nest: cavity; female lines an old woodpecker cavity or a nest box in a tree; 1 brood per year

Eggs: 10–15; creamy white without markings

Incubation: 28–36 days; female incubates

Fledging: 56–68 days; female teaches the young to feed

Migration: non-migrator in most of Oklahoma

Food: aquatic insects, plants, seeds

Compare: The female Mallard (p. 185) and female Blue-winged Teal (p. 173) lack the eye-ring and crest. The female Northern Shoveler (p. 183) is larger and has a large spoon-shaped bill.

Stan's Notes: A common duck of quiet, shallow backwater ponds. Nests in a tree cavity or a nest box in a tree. Seen flying in forests or perching on high branches. Female takes off with a loud, squealing call and enters the nest cavity from full flight. Lays some eggs in a neighboring nest (egg dumping), resulting in more than 20 eggs in some clutches. Hatchlings stay in the nest for 24 hours, then jump from as high as 60 feet (18 m) to the ground or water to follow their mother. They never return to the nest.

American Wigeon
Mareca americana

Size: 18–20" (48 cm)

Male: Brown duck with a rounded head and obvious white cap. Deep-green patch starting behind the eyes and streaking down the neck. Long pointed tail. Short, black-tipped, grayish bill. White belly and wing linings, seen in flight. Non-breeding lacks white cap and green patch.

Female: light brown with a pale-gray head, a short, black-tipped grayish bill, green wing patch (speculum) and dark eye spot; white belly and wing linings, seen in flight

Juvenile: similar to female

Nest: ground; female builds; 1 brood per year

Eggs: 7–12; white without markings

Incubation: 23–25 days; female incubates

Fledging: 37–48 days; female teaches the young to feed

Migration: complete, to Oklahoma, other southern states

Food: aquatic plants, seeds

Compare: Male American Wigeon is easily identified by the white cap and black-tipped grayish bill. Look for the black-tipped grayish bill and green wing patch to help identify the female American Wigeon.

Stan's Notes: Often in small flocks or with other ducks. Prefers shallow lakes. Male stays with the female only during the first week of incubation. Female raises the young. If threatened, female feigns injury while the young run and hide. Conceals nest in tall vegetation within 50–250 yards (46–229 m) of water.

male
p. 249

female

Gadwall
Mareca strepera

Size: 19" (48 cm)

Female: Mottled brown with a pronounced color change from dark-brown body to light-brown neck and head. Bright-white wing linings, seen in flight. Small white wing patch, seen when swimming. Gray bill with orange sides.

Male: plump gray duck with a brown head and distinctive black rump, white belly, bright-white wing linings, small white wing patch, chestnut-tinged wings, gray bill

Juvenile: similar to female

Nest: ground; female lines the nest with fine grass and down feathers plucked from her chest; 1 brood per year

Eggs: 8–11; white without markings

Incubation: 24–27 days; female incubates

Fledging: 48–56 days; young feed themselves

Migration: complete, to Oklahoma, southern states, and Mexico

Food: aquatic plants and insects

Compare: Female Mallard (p. 185) is similar but has a blue-and-white wing mark. Look for Gadwall's white wing patch and gray bill with orange sides.

Stan's Notes: A duck of shallow marshes. Consumes mostly plant material, dunking its head in water to feed rather than tipping forward, like other dabbling ducks. Walks well on land; feeds in fields and woodlands. Nests within 300 feet (90 m) of water. Often in pairs with other duck species. Establishes pair bond during winter.

male p. 267

female

Northern Shoveler
Anas clypeata

Size: 19–21" (48–53 cm)

Female: A medium-sized brown duck speckled with black. Green patch on the wings (speculum). An extraordinarily large, spoon-shaped bill.

Male: iridescent green head, rusty sides, white chest, and a large spoon-shaped bill

Juvenile: same as female

Nest: ground; female builds; 1 brood per year

Eggs: 9–12; olive without markings

Incubation: 22–25 days; female incubates

Fledging: 30–60 days; female leads the young to food

Migration: complete, to Oklahoma, southern states, Mexico, and Central America

Food: aquatic insects, plants

Compare: Female Mallard (p. 185) is similar but lacks the Shoveler's large bill. Female Wood Duck (p. 177) is smaller and has a white eye-ring. Look for Shoveler's large spoon-shaped bill to help identify.

Stan's Notes: One of several species of shovelers. Called "Shoveler" due to the peculiar, shovel-like shape of its bill. Given the common name "Northern" because it is the only species of these ducks in North America. Seen in shallow wetlands, ponds and small lakes in flocks of 5–10 birds. Flocks fly in tight formation. Swims low in water, pointing its large bill toward the water as if it's too heavy to lift. Usually swims in tight circles while feeding. Feeds mainly by filtering tiny aquatic insects and plants from the surface of the water with its bill.

male
p. 265

female

Mallard
Anas platyrhynchos

YEAR-ROUND

Size: 19–21" (48–53 cm)

Female: Brown duck with a blue-and-white wing mark (speculum). Orange-and-black bill.

Male: large green head, white necklace, rust-brown or chestnut chest, combination of gray-and-white sides, yellow bill, orange legs and feet

Juvenile: same as female but with a yellow bill

Nest: ground; female builds; 1 brood per year

Eggs: 7–10; greenish to whitish, unmarked

Incubation: 26–30 days; female incubates

Fledging: 42–52 days; female leads the young to food

Migration: non-migrator to partial in Oklahoma

Food: seeds, plants, aquatic insects; will come to ground feeders offering corn

Compare: Female Gadwall (p. 181) has a gray bill with orange sides. Female Northern Pintail (p. 187) is similar to female Mallard, but it has a gray bill. Female Northern Shoveler (p. 183) has a spoon-shaped bill. Female Wood Duck (p. 177) has a white eye-ring.

Stan's Notes: A familiar dabbling duck of lakes and ponds. Also found in rivers, streams, and some backyards. Tips forward to feed on vegetation on the bottom of shallow water. The name "Mallard" comes from the Latin word *masculus,* meaning "male," referring to the male's habit of taking no part in raising the young. Female and male have white underwings and white tails, but only the male has black central tail feathers that curl upward. The female gives a classic quack. Returns to its birthplace each year.

Northern Pintail
Anas acuta

YEAR-ROUND
WINTER

Size: 20" (52 cm), female
25" (63 cm), male

Male: A slender, elegant duck with a brown head, white neck and gray body. Gray bill. Extremely long and narrow black tail. Non-breeding has a pale-brown head that lacks the clear demarcation between the brown head and white neck. Lacks long tail feathers.

Female: mottled brown body with a paler head and neck, long tail, gray bill

Juvenile: similar to female

Nest: ground; female builds; 1 brood per year

Eggs: 6–9; olive-green without markings

Incubation: 22–25 days; female incubates

Fledging: 36–50 days; female teaches young to feed

Migration: partial to non-migrator, to Oklahoma, southern states, and Mexico

Food: aquatic plants and insects, seeds

Compare: The male Northern Pintail has a distinctive brown head and white neck and unique long tail feathers. Female Mallard (p. 185) is similar to female Pintail, but Mallard has an orange bill with black spots.

Stan's Notes: A common dabbling duck of alkaline marshes. About 90 percent of its diet is aquatic plants, except when females feed heavily on aquatic insects prior to nesting, presumably to gain extra nutrients for egg production. Male molts in the winter, appearing more like female. Male holds tail upright from the water's surface. No other North American duck has such a long tail. Flies in line formation.

female

male
p. 247

soaring

Northern Harrier
Circus hudsonius

Size: 18–22" (45–56 cm); up to 4' wingspan

Female: Slender, low-flying hawk with a dark-brown back and brown streaking on the chest and belly. Large white rump patch. Thin black tail bands and black wing tips. Yellow eyes.

Male: silver-gray with a large white rump patch and white belly, black wing tips, yellow eyes, faint, thin bands across the tail

Juvenile: similar to female, with an orange breast

Nest: ground; female and male construct; 1 brood per year

Eggs: 4–8; bluish white without markings

Incubation: 31–32 days; female incubates

Fledging: 30–35 days; male and female feed the young

Migration: partial migrator, to southern states, Mexico, and Central America; non-migrator in northern half of Oklahoma

Food: mice, snakes, insects, small birds

Compare: Slimmer than the Red-tailed Hawk (p. 193). Look for the characteristic low gliding and the black tail bands to identify the female Harrier.

Stan's Notes: One of the easiest of hawks to identify. Glides just above the ground, following the contours of the land while searching for prey. Holds its wings just above horizontal, tilting back and forth in the wind, similar to the Turkey Vulture. Formerly called Marsh Hawk due to its habit of hunting over marshes. Feeds and nests on the ground. Will also preen and rest on the ground. Unlike other hawks, mainly uses its hearing to find prey, followed by its sight. At any age, it has a distinctive owl-like face disk.

soaring light morph

intermediate morph

light morph

dark morph

soaring dark morph

Swainson's Hawk
Buteo swainsoni

SUMMER MIGRATION

Size: 19–22" (48–56 cm); up to 4¾' wingspan

Male: Highly variable plumage with three easily distinguishable color morphs. Light morph is brown and has a white belly, warm rusty chest, and white face. Intermediate has a dark chest, rusty belly, and white at the base of bill. Dark morph is nearly all dark brown with a rusty color low on the belly.

Female: same as male

Juvenile: similar to adult

Nest: platform; female and male construct; 1 brood per year

Eggs: 2–4; bluish or white with some brown marks

Incubation: 28–35 days; female and male incubate

Fledging: 28–30 days; female and male feed young

Migration: complete, to Central and South America

Food: small mammals, insects, snakes, birds

Compare: Slimmer than Red-tailed Hawk (p. 193), which has a white chest and brown belly band. Swainson's Hawk has longer, more pointed wings and a longer tail.

Stan's Notes: A slender open country hawk that hunts mammals, insects, snakes, and birds when soaring (kiting) or perching. Often flies with slightly upturned wings in a teetering, vulture-like flight. The light morph is the most common, but the intermediate and dark are also common. Even minor nest disturbance can cause nest failure. Often gathers in large flocks to migrate.

soaring

juvenile
soaring

juvenile

Red-tailed Hawk

Buteo jamaicensis

Size: 19–23" (48–63 cm); up to 4½' wingspan

Male: Variety of colorations, from chocolate brown to nearly all white. Often brown with a white breast and brown belly band. Rust-red tail. Underside of wing is white with a small dark patch on the leading edge near the shoulder.

Female: same as male but slightly larger

Juvenile: similar to adults, with a speckled breast and light eyes; lacks a red tail

Nest: platform; male and female build; 1 brood per year

Eggs: 2–3; white without markings or sometimes marked with brown

Incubation: 30–35 days; female and male incubate

Fledging: 45–46 days; male and female feed the young

Migration: non-migrator to partial migrator; moves around to find food

Food: small and medium-sized animals, large birds, snakes, fish, insects, bats, carrion

Compare: Swainson's Hawk (p. 191) is slimmer with longer, more pointed wings.

Stan's Notes: Common in open country and cities. Seen perching on fences, freeway lampposts, and trees. Look for it circling above open fields and roadsides, searching for prey. Gives a high-pitched scream that trails off. Often builds a large stick nest in large trees along roads. Lines nest with finer material, like evergreen needles. Returns to the same nest site each year. The red tail develops in the second year and is best seen from above.

Barred Owl
Strix varia

Size: 20–24" (51–61 cm); up to 3½' wingspan

Male: Chunky brown-and-gray owl. Dark horizontal barring on upper chest. Vertical streaks on lower chest and belly. A large head and dark-brown eyes. Yellow bill and feet.

Female: same as male but slightly larger

Juvenile: light gray with a black face

Nest: cavity; does not add any nesting material; 1 brood per year

Eggs: 2–3; white without markings

Incubation: 28–33 days; female incubates

Fledging: 42–44 days; female and male feed the young

Migration: non-migrator

Food: mice, rabbits and other animals; small birds; fish; reptiles; amphibians

Compare: Great Horned Owl (p. 197) has "horns," and the much smaller Eastern Screech-Owl (p. 225) has ears, both of which Barred Owl lacks. Look for a stocky owl with a large head and dark-brown eyes to identify the Barred Owl.

Stan's Notes: A very common owl, often seen hunting during the day. Perches and watches for mice, birds, and other prey. Hovers over water and reaches down to grab fish. Prefers deciduous, dense woodlands with sparse undergrowth, but it can be attracted to your yard with a simple nest box that has a large entrance hole. After fledging, the young stay with their parents for up to four months. Often sounds similar to a dog barking just before calling six to eight hoots, sounding like "who-who-who-cooks-for-you."

Great Horned Owl
Bubo virginianus

Size: 21–25" (53–64 cm); up to 4' wingspan

Male: Robust brown "horned" owl. Bright-yellow eyes and a V-shaped white throat resembling a necklace. Horizontal barring on the chest.

Female: same as male but slightly larger

Juvenile: similar to adults but lacks ear tufts

Nest: no nest; takes over the nest of a crow, hawk, or Great Blue Heron or uses a partial cavity, stump, or broken tree; 1 brood per year

Eggs: 2–3; white without markings

Incubation: 26–30 days; female incubates

Fledging: 30–35 days; male and female feed the young

Migration: non-migrator

Food: mammals, birds (ducks), snakes, insects

Compare: Burrowing Owl (p. 147) is much smaller and has long legs. The Barred Owl (p. 195) has dark eyes and no "horns." Look for bright-yellow eyes and feather "horns" on the head to help identify the Great Horned Owl.

Stan's Notes: The largest resident owl in the state. One of the earliest nesters in Oklahoma, laying eggs in January and February. Able to hunt in complete darkness due to its excellent hearing. The "horns," or "ears," are tufts of feathers and have nothing to do with hearing. Cannot turn its head all the way around. Wing feathers are ragged on the ends, resulting in silent flight. Eyelids close from the top down, like humans. Fearless, it is one of the few animals that will kill skunks and porcupines. Given that, it is also called the Flying Tiger. Call sounds like "hoo-hoo-hoo-hoooo."

displaying

Greater Roadrunner

Geococcyx californianus

Size: 23" (58 cm)

Male: Overall brown with white streaking. Long, pointed brown bill. Extremely long tail. Blue patch just behind eyes. Short round wings are darker brown than body. Long gray legs with large feet. Has a conspicuous crest that can be raised and lowered.

Female: same as male

Juvenile: similar to adult

Nest: platform, low in a tree, shrub or cactus; the female and male build; 1–2 broods per year

Eggs: 4–6; white without markings

Incubation: 18–20 days; male and female incubate

Fledging: 16–18 days; male and female feed young

Migration: non-migrator

Food: insects, reptiles, small mammals, and birds

Compare: This uniquely shaped ground dweller has an extremely long tail, a prominent crest, and is hard to confuse with other birds. Closely related to the tree-dwelling Yellow-billed Cuckoo (p. 163), but little resemblance.

Stan's Notes: Ground dweller with a very long tail and prominent crest when raised. Cuckoo family member known to run quickly across the ground to catch prey. A formidable predator, able to run up to 15 miles (24 km) per hour. Flies short distances, usually in a low glide after a running takeoff. Raises its tail high, lowers it slowly. A slow, descending, low-pitched "coo-coo-coo-coo." Male does most incubating and feeding of young. Performs a distraction display to protect the nest. Young can catch prey four weeks after leaving the nest.

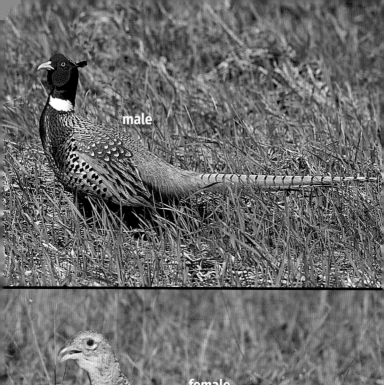

male

female

Ring-necked Pheasant
Phasianus colchicus

YEAR-ROUND

Size: 30–36" (76–91 cm), male, including tail
21–25" (53–64 cm), female, including tail

Male: Golden-brown body with a long tail. White ring around the neck. Head is purple, green, blue, and red.

Female: smaller and less flamboyant than the male, with brown plumage and a long tail

Juvenile: similar to female, with a shorter tail

Nest: ground; female builds; 1 brood per year

Eggs: 8–10; olive-brown without markings

Incubation: 23–25 days; female incubates

Fledging: 11–12 days; female leads the young to food

Migration: non-migrator

Food: insects, seeds, fruit; visits ground feeders

Compare: Male and female Pheasants have long tails, but the male is brightly colored.

Stan's Notes: Originally introduced to North America from China in the late 1800s. Common now throughout the U.S. Like many other game birds, its numbers vary greatly, making it common in some years, scarce in others. Seeks shelter during harsh winter weather. To attract females, the male gives a cackling call and then rapidly flutters his wings. Takes off in an explosive flight with fast wingbeats followed by gliding low to the ground. The name "Ring-necked" refers to the white ring around the male's neck. "Pheasant" comes from the Greek word *phaisianos*, which means "bird of the River Phasis" (known today as the Rioni River).

displaying male

non-displaying

female

Wild Turkey
Meleagris gallopavo

Size: 36–48" (91–122 cm)

Male: Large brown-and-bronze bird with a naked blue-and-red head. Long, straight, black beard in the center of the chest. Tail spreads open like a fan. Spurs on legs.

Female: thinner and less striking than the male; often lacks a breast beard

Juvenile: same as adult of the same sex

Nest: ground; female builds; 1 brood per year

Eggs: 10–12; buff-white with dull-brown markings

Incubation: 27–28 days; female incubates

Fledging: 6–10 days; female leads the young to food

Migration: non-migrator; moves around to find food

Food: insects, seeds, fruit

Compare: This bird is quite distinctive and unlikely to be confused with others.

Stan's Notes: The largest game bird in the state and the species from which the domestic turkey was bred. A strong flier that can approach 60 miles (97 km) per hour. Can fly straight up, then away. Eyesight is three times better than ours. Hearing is also excellent; can hear competing males up to a mile away. Male has a "harem" of up to 20 females. Female scrapes out a shallow depression for nesting and pads it with soft leaves. Males are known as toms, females are hens, and young are poults. Roosts in trees at night.

Ruby-crowned Kinglet
Regulus calendula

MIGRATION
WINTER

Size: 4" (10 cm)

Male: Small, teardrop-shaped green-to-gray bird. Two white wing bars and a white eye-ring. Hidden ruby crown.

Female: same as male, but lacks a ruby crown

Juvenile: same as female

Nest: pendulous; female builds; 1 brood per year

Eggs: 4–5; white with brown markings

Incubation: 11–12 days; female incubates

Fledging: 11–12 days; female and male feed the young

Migration: complete, to southern states, Mexico, and Central America; winters in Oklahoma

Food: insects, berries

Compare: The female American Goldfinch (p. 299) shares the drab olive plumage and unmarked chest, but it is larger. Look for the white eye-ring to identify the Ruby-crowned Kinglet.

Stan's Notes: This is one of the smaller birds in Oklahoma. Seen during migration, look for it flitting around thick shrubs low to the ground. It takes a quick eye to see the ruby crown, which the male flashes when he is excited. The female weaves an unusually intricate nest and fastens colorful lichens and mosses to the exterior with spiderwebs. Often builds the nest high in a mature tree, where it hangs from a branch that has overlapping leaves. Sings a distinctive song that starts out soft and ends loud and on a higher note. "Kinglet" originates from the word *king,* referring to the male's red crown, and the diminutive suffix *let,* meaning "small."

Red-breasted Nuthatch
Sitta canadensis

WINTER

Size: 4½" (11 cm)

Male: Gray-backed bird with an obvious black eye line and black cap. Rust-red breast and belly.

Female: duller than male and has a gray cap and pale undersides

Juvenile: same as female

Nest: cavity; male and female excavate a cavity or move into a vacant hole; 1 brood per year

Eggs: 5–6; white with red-brown markings

Incubation: 11–12 days; female incubates

Fledging: 14–20 days; female and male feed the young

Migration: irruptive; moves around the state in search of food in winter

Food: insects, insect eggs, seeds; comes to seed and suet feeders

Compare: White-breasted Nuthatch (p. 211) is larger and does not have the rust-red breast and black eye line of Red-breasted Nuthatch.

Stan's Notes: The nuthatch climbs down trunks of trees headfirst, searching for insects. Like a chickadee, it grabs a seed from a feeder and flies off to crack it open. It wedges the seed into a crevice and pounds it open with several sharp blows. The name "Nuthatch" comes from the Middle English moniker *nuthak*, referring to the habit of hacking seeds open. Look for it in mature conifers, where it extracts seeds from pine cones. Excavates a cavity or takes an old woodpecker hole or a natural cavity and builds a nest within. Gives a series of nasal "yank-yank-yank" calls. A winter visitor in Oklahoma that is more abundant in some years and absent in others.

Carolina Chickadee
Poecile carolinensis

Size: 5" (13 cm)

Male: Mostly gray with a black cap and chin. White face and chest with a tan belly. Darker-gray tail.

Female: same as male

Juvenile: same as adult

Nest: cavity; female and male build or excavate; 1–2 broods per year

Eggs: 5–7; white with reddish brown markings

Incubation: 11–12 days; female and male incubate

Fledging: 13–17 days; female and male feed the young

Migration: non-migrator

Food: insects, seeds, fruit; comes to seed and suet feeders

Compare: Tufted Titmouse (p. 217) is a close relative, but it has an erect crest and lacks the black cap and chin.

Stan's Notes: A common bird in Oklahoma. One of the first birds to use a newly placed feeder. Flies to a feeder, grabs a seed, and carries it to a branch. To get to the meat inside, it holds the seed down with its feet and hammers the shell open with its bill. Returns for another seed. A friendly bird. Can be tamed and hand-fed. Attracted with a nest box that has a 1¼-inch entrance hole. Female gives a loud snake-like hiss if disturbed on the nest. Often seen with other birds (mixed flock) in winter. Song is a high, fast "chika-dee-dee-dee-dee."

male

female

White-breasted Nuthatch
Sitta carolinensis

YEAR-ROUND

Size: 5–6" (13–15 cm)

Male: Slate gray with a white face, breast, and belly. Large white patch on the rump. Black cap and nape. Bill is long and thin, slightly upturned. Chestnut undertail.

Female: similar to male, but has a gray cap and nape

Juvenile: similar to female

Nest: cavity; female and male build a nest within; 1 brood per year

Eggs: 5–7; white with brown markings

Incubation: 11–12 days; female incubates

Fledging: 13–14 days; female and male feed the young

Migration: non-migrator

Food: insects, insect eggs, seeds; comes to seed and suet feeders

Compare: Red-breasted Nuthatch (p. 207) is smaller and has a rust-red belly and distinctive black eye line.

Stan's Notes: The nuthatch hops headfirst down trees, looking for insects missed by birds climbing up. Its climbing agility is due to an extra-long hind toe claw, or nail, that is nearly twice the size of its front claws. "Nuthatch," from the Middle English *nuthak*, refers to the bird's habit of wedging a seed in a crevice and hacking it open. Often seen in flocks with chickadees and Downy Woodpeckers. Mates stay together year-round, defending a small territory. Gives a characteristic "whi-whi-whi-whi" spring call during February and March. One of nearly 30 worldwide nuthatch species.

male

female

first winter

Yellow-rumped Warbler
Setophaga coronata

MIGRATION
WINTER

Size: 5–6" (13–15 cm)

Male: Slate gray with black streaking on the chest. Yellow patches on the head, flanks, and rump. White chin and belly. Two white wing bars.

Female: duller gray than the male, mixed with brown

Juvenile: first winter is similar to the adult female

Nest: cup; female builds; 2 broods per year

Eggs: 4–5; white with brown markings

Incubation: 12–13 days; female incubates

Fledging: 10–12 days; female and male feed young

Migration: complete, to Oklahoma, southern states, Mexico, and Central America

Food: insects, berries; visits suet feeders in spring

Compare: The male Common Yellowthroat (p. 301) has a yellow chest and distinctive black mask. The male Yellow Warbler (p. 303) is all yellow with orange streaks on breast. Look for patches of yellow on the rump, head, flanks, and chin of Yellow-rumped Warbler to help identify.

Stan's Notes: A common wintering warbler in Oklahoma, it is one of the few to spend the winter. Flocks of hundreds seen during migration. Usually arrives in late September to early October. By November, very few are found in the Panhandle. Familiar call is a single robust "chip," heard mostly during migration. Sings a wonderful song in spring. Builds nest in coniferous and aspen forests, but doesn't nest in Oklahoma. In the fall, the male molts to a dull color similar to the female, but he retains his yellow patches all year. Frequently called Myrtle Warbler in eastern states and Audubon's Warbler in western states. Sometimes called Butterbutt due to the yellow patch on its rump.

female
p. 101

male

Dark-eyed Junco
Junco hyemalis

WINTER

Size: 5½" (14 cm)

Male: Plump, dark-eyed bird with a slate-gray-to-charcoal chest, head, and back. White belly. Pink bill. White outer tail feathers appear like a white V in flight.

Female: round with brown plumage

Juvenile: similar to female, with streaking on the breast and head

Nest: cup; female and male build; 2 broods per year

Eggs: 3–5; white with reddish-brown markings

Incubation: 12–13 days; female incubates

Fledging: 10–13 days; male and female feed the young

Migration: complete, throughout the U.S.; winters in Oklahoma

Food: seeds, insects; visits ground and seed feeders

Compare: Rarely confused with any other bird. Look for the pink bill and small flocks feeding under feeders to identify the male Dark-eyed Junco.

Stan's Notes: Common in winter, this bird is usually seen on the ground in small flocks. Adheres to a rigid social hierarchy, with dominant birds chasing the less dominant birds. Look for the white outer tail feathers flashing in flight. Most comfortable on the ground, juncos will use their feet to simultaneously "double-scratch" to expose seeds and insects. Eats many weed seeds. Several sub-species of Dark-eyed Junco were previously considered to be separate species but have now been combined into one. Constructs nest in a wide variety of wooded habitats. Doesn't nest in Oklahoma.

Tufted Titmouse

Baeolophus bicolor

YEAR-ROUND

Size: 6" (15 cm)

Male: Slate gray with a white chest and belly. Pointed crest. Rust-brown wash on the flanks. Gray legs and dark eyes.

Female: same as male

Juvenile: same as adult

Nest: cavity; female lines an old woodpecker cavity; 2 broods per year

Eggs: 5–7; white with brown markings

Incubation: 13–14 days; female incubates

Fledging: 15–18 days; female and male feed the young

Migration: non-migrator

Food: insects, seeds, fruit; will come to seed and suet feeders

Compare: The Carolina Chickadee (p. 209) is a close relative but is smaller and lacks a crest. The White-breasted Nuthatch (p. 211) has a rust-brown undertail. Look for the pointed crest to help identify the Tufted Titmouse.

Stan's Notes: A common feeder bird that can be attracted with an offering of black oil sunflower seeds or suet. Can also be attracted with a nest box. Well known for its "peter-peter-peter" call, which it quickly repeats. Notorious for pulling hair from sleeping dogs, cats, and squirrels to line its nest. Usually seen only one or two at a time. Male feeds female during courtship and nesting. The prefix *tit* in the common name comes from a Scandinavian word meaning "little." Suffix *mouse* is derived from the Old English word *mase*, meaning "bird." Simply translated, it is a "small bird."

Eastern Phoebe

Sayornis phoebe

Size: 7" (18 cm)

Male: Plain gray with slightly darker wings and a light-olive belly. Thin, dark bill.

Female: same as male

Juvenile: same as adults

Nest: cup; female builds; 2 broods per year

Eggs: 4–5; white without markings

Incubation: 15–16 days; female incubates

Fledging: 15–16 days; male and female feed the young

Migration: complete, to southern states and Mexico; non-migrator in parts of Oklahoma

Food: insects

Compare: The Gray Catbird (p. 227) has a black crown and a chestnut patch under its tail. Eastern Phoebe lacks any distinctive markings. Listen for its well-enunciated "fee-bee" call and look for the hawking and tail-pumping behaviors to help identify this bird.

Stan's Notes: A sparrow-sized bird that often perches on the end of a dead branch. Found in forests, yards, and farms. In a process called hawking, it waits for a passing insect. When a bug flies near, it launches out to catch it and then returns to the same branch. It has a distinctive habit of pumping its tail up and down while perching. Builds nest beneath the eaves of houses, under bridges or in other sheltered spots. Uses mud, grass, and moss for nest materials and hair (and sometimes feathers) for the lining. The common name is derived from its distinct "fee-bee" call, which it repeats over and over from the top of dead branches.

Great Crested Flycatcher
Myiarchus crinitus

SUMMER
MIGRATION

Size: 8" (20 cm)

Male: Gray head with a prominent crest. Gray back and throat. Yellow from the belly to the base of a reddish-brown tail. Lower bill is yellow at the base.

Female: same as male

Juvenile: same as adults

Nest: cavity; female and male stuff a vacant woodpecker cavity or nest box; 1 brood per year

Eggs: 4–6; white to buff with brown markings

Incubation: 13–15 days; female incubates

Fledging: 14–21 days; female and male feed the young

Migration: complete, to Mexico and Central America

Food: insects, fruit

Compare: The Eastern Kingbird (p. 223) has a white band across its tail. The Eastern Phoebe (p. 219) is similar, but it lacks a crest and yellow belly. Look for the crest to identify the Flycatcher.

Stan's Notes: Breeds throughout most of Oklahoma. A common bird of almost any wooded area, it lives high up in trees, rarely coming to the ground. Makes long flights from treetop to treetop, moving from one hunting area to another. Gleans insects from tree leaves. Often heard before seen. "Great Crested" refers to the set of extra-long feathers on top of its head (crest), which the bird raises when alert or agitated, like the Northern Cardinal. Nests in an old woodpecker hole but can be attracted with a man-made nest box that has an entrance hole 1½–2½ inches (4–6 cm) in diameter. Often stuffs the cavity with a collection of fur, feathers, string, and snake skins.

Eastern Kingbird
Tyrannus tyrannus

SUMMER
MIGRATION

Size: 8" (20 cm)

Male: Mostly gray and black with a white chin and belly. Black head and tail with a distinct white band on the tip of the tail. Concealed red crown, rarely seen.

Female: same as male

Juvenile: same as adults

Nest: cup; male and female build; 1 brood per year

Eggs: 3–4; white with brown markings

Incubation: 16–18 days; female incubates

Fledging: 16–18 days; female and male feed the young

Migration: complete, to Mexico, Central America, and South America

Food: insects, fruit

Compare: American Robin (p. 231) is larger and has a rust-red breast. Western Kingbird (p. 313) is yellow on the belly and under the wings. Look for the white band along the end of the tail to identify.

Stan's Notes: Common bird throughout Oklahoma in open fields and prairies. Autumn migration begins in late August and early September. As many as 20 birds migrate in a group. Returns to the mating ground in spring, where pairs defend their territory. Seems to be unafraid of other birds and chases larger birds. Given the common name "King" for its bold attitude and behavior. In a hunting technique known as hawking, it perches on a branch and watches for insects, flies out to catch one, and then returns to the same perch. Swoops from perch to perch when hunting. Becomes very vocal during late summer, when family members call back and forth to one another while hunting for insects.

red morph

gray morph

Eastern Screech-Owl
Megascops asio

YEAR-ROUND

Size: 8–10" (20–25 cm); up to 2' wingspan

Male: Small "eared" owl that occurs in different colorations. Gray morph is mottled gray and white. Red morph is mottled rust and white. Short wings. Bright-yellow eyes.

Female: same as male but slightly larger

Juvenile: lighter color than adults of the same morph and usually lacks ear tufts

Nest: cavity, old woodpecker cavity or man-made nest box; does not add any nesting material; 1 brood per year

Eggs: 4–5; white without markings

Incubation: 25–26 days; female incubates, male feeds the female during incubation

Fledging: 26–27 days; male and female feed the young

Migration: non-migrator; moves around in winter

Food: large insects, small mammals, birds, snakes

Compare: This is the only small owl in Oklahoma with ear tufts. Can be gray or rust in color.

Stan's Notes: Commonly found in forests that have suitable natural cavities for nesting and roosting. Active from dusk to dawn. Usually gives a tremulous, descending trill, like a sound effect in a scary movie. Seldom gives a screeching call. Often seen sunning itself at a nest-box hole during winter. Mates may have a long-term pair bond and may roost together at night. Excellent hearing and eyesight. Flaps rapidly and flies silently. Has winter and summer territories. The gray morph is more common than the red.

Gray Catbird
Dumetella carolinensis

SUMMER MIGRATION

Size: 9" (23 cm)

Male: Handsome slate-gray bird with a black crown and a long, thin black bill. Often lifts up its tail, exposing a chestnut patch beneath.

Female: same as male

Juvenile: same as adults

Nest: cup; female and male build; 2 broods per year

Eggs: 4–6; blue-green without markings

Incubation: 12–13 days; female incubates

Fledging: 10–11 days; female and male feed the young

Migration: complete, to southern states

Food: insects, occasional fruit; visits suet feeders

Compare: The Eastern Phoebe (p. 219) is smaller and has an olive belly. The Eastern Kingbird (p. 223) is similar in size but has a white belly and a white band across its tail. To identify the Gray Catbird, look for the black crown and chestnut patch under the tail.

Stan's Notes: Returns to the state by the last week of April. Seen in great numbers during fall migration in the last week of September and in early October. A secretive bird, more often heard than seen. The Chippewa Indians gave it a name that means "the bird that cries with grief" due to its raspy call. Called "Catbird" because the sound is like the meowing of a house cat. Often mimics other birds, rarely repeating the same phrases. Found in forest edges, backyards, and parks. Builds its nest with small twigs. Nests in thick shrubs and quickly flies back into shrubs if approached. If a cowbird lays an egg in its nest, the catbird will quickly break it and eject it.

Loggerhead Shrike
Lanius ludovicianus

Size: 9" (22.5 cm)

Male: Gray head and back and a white chin, breast, and belly. Black wings, tail, legs, and feet. Black mask across the eyes and a black bill with a hooked tip. White wing patches, seen in flight.

Female: same as male

Juvenile: dull version of adult

Nest: cup; male and female construct; 1–2 broods per year

Eggs: 4–7; off-white with dark markings

Incubation: 16–17 days; female incubates

Fledging: 17–21 days; female and male feed the young

Migration: complete, to southern states; non-migrator in Oklahoma

Food: insects, lizards, small mammals, frogs

Compare: Northern Mockingbird (p. 233) has a similar color pattern, but lacks the black mask of the Loggerhead. Shrike is stockier than the Mockingbird and perches in more open places. Look for the black wings and mask across the eyes to help identify it.

Stan's Notes: The Loggerhead is a songbird that acts like a bird of prey. Known for skewering prey on barbed wire fences, thorns, and other sharp objects to store or hold still while tearing apart to eat, hence its other common name, Butcher Bird. Feet are too weak to hold the prey it eats. Breeding bird surveys indicate declining populations in the Great Plains due to pesticides killing its major food source—grasshoppers. Stable populations, however, in Oklahoma.

male

female

American Robin
Turdus migratorius

YEAR-ROUND

Size: 9–11" (23–28 cm)

Male: Familiar gray bird with a dark rust-red breast and a nearly black head and tail. White chin with black streaks. White eye-ring.

Female: similar to male, with a duller rust-red breast and a gray head

Juvenile: similar to female, with a speckled breast and brown back

Nest: cup; female builds with help from the male; 2–3 broods per year

Eggs: 4–7; pale blue without markings

Incubation: 12–14 days; female incubates

Fledging: 14–16 days; female and male feed the young

Migration: complete, to southern states, Mexico, and Central America; non-migrator in Oklahoma

Food: insects, fruit, berries, earthworms

Compare: Familiar bird to all. To differentiate the male from the female, compare the nearly black head and rust-red chest of the male with the gray head and duller chest of the female.

Stan's Notes: Although complete migrators in northern states, the robin is a year-round resident in Oklahoma. Can be heard singing all night long in spring. City robins sing louder than country robins in order to hear one another over traffic and noise. A robin isn't listening for worms when it turns its head to one side. It is focusing its sight out of one eye to look for dirt moving, which is caused by worms moving. Territorial, often fighting its reflection in a window.

displaying

Northern Mockingbird
Mimus polyglottos

YEAR-ROUND

Size: 10" (25 cm)

Male: Silvery-gray head and back with a light-gray breast and belly. White wing patches, seen in flight or during display. Tail mostly black with white outer tail feathers. Black bill.

Female: same as male

Juvenile: dull gray with a heavily streaked breast and a gray bill

Nest: cup; female and male construct; 2 broods per year, sometimes more

Eggs: 3–5; blue-green with brown markings

Incubation: 12–13 days; female incubates

Fledging: 11–13 days; female and male feed the young

Migration: partial migrator, to southern states; non-migrator in Oklahoma

Food: insects, fruit

Compare: Loggerhead Shrike (p. 229) has a similar color pattern but is stockier, has a black mask, and perches in more open spaces. The Gray Catbird (p. 227) is slate gray and lacks wing patches. Look for the Mockingbird to spread its wings, flash its white wing patches, and wag its tail from side to side.

Stan's Notes: A very animated bird. Performs an elaborate mating dance. Facing each other with heads and tails erect, pairs will run toward each other, flashing their white wing patches, and then retreat to cover nearby. Thought to flash the wing patches to scare up insects when hunting. Sits for long periods on top of shrubs. Imitates other birds (vocal mimicry), hence the common name. Young males often sing at night.

Eurasian Collared-Dove
Streptopelia decaocto

YEAR-ROUND

Size: 12½" (32 cm)

Male: Head, neck, breast, and belly are gray to tan. Back, wings, and tail are slightly darker. Thin black collar with a white border on the nape of the neck. Tail is long and squared.

Female: same as male

Juvenile: similar to adults

Nest: platform; female and male build; 2–3 broods per year

Eggs: 3–5; creamy white without markings

Incubation: 12–14 days; female and male incubate

Fledging: 15–20 days; female and male feed the young

Migration: non-migrator

Food: seeds; will visit ground and seed feeders

Compare: The Mourning Dove (p. 165) is slightly smaller and darker. The Rock Pigeon (p. 237) has colorful iridescent patches. Look for the black collar on the nape and the squared tail to help identify the Eurasian Collared-Dove.

Stan's Notes: It has been expanding its range across North America and is predicted to spread just like it did through Europe from Asia. Unknown how this "new" bird will affect populations of the native Mourning Dove. Nearly identical to the Ringed Turtle-Dove, a common pet bird. The dark mark on the back of the neck gave rise to the common name. Look for flashes of white in the tail and dark wing tips when it lands or takes off.

Rock Pigeon
Columba livia

YEAR-ROUND

Size: 13" (33 cm)

Male: No set color pattern. Shades of gray to white with patches of gleaming, iridescent green and blue. Often has a light rump patch.

Female: same as male

Juvenile: same as adults

Nest: platform; female builds; 3–4 broods per year

Eggs: 1–2; white without markings

Incubation: 18–20 days; female and male incubate

Fledging: 25–26 days; female and male feed the young

Migration: non-migrator

Food: seeds

Compare: The Eurasian Collared-Dove (p. 235) has a black collar on the nape. The Mourning Dove (p. 165) is smaller and light brown and lacks the variety of color combinations of the Rock Pigeon.

Stan's Notes: Also known as the Domestic Pigeon. Formerly known as the Rock Dove. Introduced to North America from Europe by the early settlers. Most common around cities and barnyards, where it scratches for seeds. One of the few birds with a wide variety of colors, produced by years of selective breeding while in captivity. Parents feed the young a regurgitated liquid known as crop-milk for the first few days of life. One of the few birds that can drink without tilting its head back. Nests under bridges or on buildings, balconies, barns, and sheds. Was once thought to be a nuisance in cities and was poisoned. Now, many cities have Peregrine Falcons (p. 245) feeding on Rock Pigeons, which keeps their numbers in check.

in flight

winter

breeding

Franklin's Gull
Leucophaeus pipixcan

MIGRATION

Size: 14–15" (36–38 cm); up to 3' wingspan

Male: Gray-and-white gull with a black head and black extending partially down the front of neck. Black wing tips. Large white eye-ring. Reddish bill. Winter plumage has a partial black "hood" and a mostly black bill.

Female: same as male

Juvenile: brown back, partially black head, black bill

Nest: floating platform; male and female construct; 1 brood per year

Eggs: 2–4; greenish with brown markings

Incubation: 24–25 days; female and male incubate

Fledging: 31–33 days; female and male feed the young

Migration: complete, to southern states, Mexico, Central and South America

Food: insects, fish

Compare: Black-headed gull that occurs regularly in Oklahoma during migration. Look for it in open marshes, with its black "hood" and black wing tips.

Stan's Notes: Usually seen during spring and autumn migrations, when hundreds gather in prairie lakes. A three-year gull. Juveniles have brown backs, partly black heads, and black bills. First- and second-year birds look similar to winter adults, with gray-and-white plumage, partly black heads, and black bills. Obtains adult plumage at three years. Winters on the Pacific Coast, all along Central and South America. Breeds in prairie pothole region. Doesn't nest in Oklahoma.

soaring

juvenile

Sharp-shinned Hawk
Accipiter striatus

WINTER

Size: 10–14" (25–36 cm); up to 2' wingspan

Male: Small woodland hawk with a gray back and head and a rust-red chest. Short wings. Long, squared tail and several dark tail bands, with the widest at the end of the tail. Red eyes.

Female: same as male but larger

Juvenile: same size as adults, with a brown back, heavy streaking on the chest and yellow eyes

Nest: platform; female builds; 1 brood per year

Eggs: 4–5; white with brown markings

Incubation: 32–35 days; female incubates

Fledging: 24–27 days; female and male feed the young

Migration: complete, to southern states, Mexico, and Central America; winters in Oklahoma

Food: birds, small mammals

Compare: Smallest hawk seen during winter. Smaller than the Mississippi Kite (p. 243), which is overall gray with a nearly white head. Look for the squared tail to help identify the Sharp-shinned Hawk.

Stan's Notes: A hawk of backyards, parks, and woodlands. Seen swooping on birds visiting feeders and chasing them as they flee. Its short wingspan and long tail help it to maneuver through thick stands of trees in pursuit of prey. Calls a loud, high-pitched "kik-kik-kik-kik." Named "Sharp-shinned" for the sharp projection (keel) on the leading edge of its shin. A bird's shin is actually below the ankle (rather than above it, like ours) on the tarsus bone of its foot. In most birds, the tarsus bone is rounded, not sharp.

soaring

juvenile

soaring
juvenile

Mississippi Kite
Ictinia mississippiensis

Size: 12–15" (30–38 cm); up to 2¾' wingspan

Male: Overall gray bird with a paler, nearly white head. Nearly black tail. Dark eye patch surrounding red eyes. Short, hooked gray bill. Yellow legs and feet.

Female: same as male

Juvenile: similar to adult but has a brown chest with vertical white streaks

Nest: platform; female and male build; 1 brood per year

Eggs: 1–2; white without markings

Incubation: 29–32 days; female and male incubate

Fledging: 32–34 days; female and male feed young

Migration: complete, to South America

Food: insects, lizards, small snakes

Compare: Smaller than many other birds of prey. The overall gray appearance with a lighter head makes it easy to identify.

Stan's Notes: A bird of prey that eats mostly large insects. Groups follow livestock, feeding on insects they kick up. Hunts insects by soaring or hovering, catching in flight, or diving down. It requires open areas with scattered trees for nesting. Nests in semi-colonies. Mated pairs aggressively defend nest sites. Individuals often stray out of traditional ranges, appearing in northern states and up the East Coast.

243

juvenile

in-flight
juvenile

in flight

Peregrine Falcon
Falco peregrinus

MIGRATION

Size: 16–20" (41–51 cm); up to 3¾' wingspan

Male: Dark-gray back and tan-to-white chest. Horizontal bars on belly, legs, and undertail. Dark "hood" head marking and wide black mustache. Yellow base of bill and eye-ring. Yellow legs.

Female: similar to male but noticeably larger

Juvenile: overall darker than adults, with heavy streaking on the chest and belly

Nest: ground (scrape) on a cliff edge, tall building, bridge or smokestack; 1 brood per year

Eggs: 3–4; white, some with brown markings

Incubation: 29–32 days; female and male incubate

Fledging: 35–42 days; male and female feed the young

Migration: complete, to southern states

Food: birds (Rock Pigeons in cities; shorebirds and waterfowl in rural areas)

Compare: The American Kestrel (p. 149) is smaller and has 2 vertical black stripes on its face. Look for the dark "hood" head marking and mustache marks to identify the Peregrine Falcon.

Stan's Notes: A wide-bodied raptor that hunts many bird species. The larger females hunt larger prey. Lives in many cities, diving (stooping) on pigeons at speeds of up to 200 miles (322 km) per hour, which knocks them to the ground. Soars with its wings flat, often riding thermals. During courtship, the male brings food to the female and performs aerial displays. Likes to nest on a high ledge or platform for a good view of its territory. A solitary nester and monogamous.

female
p. 189

male

soaring

Northern Harrier
Circus hudsonius

YEAR-ROUND
WINTER

Size: 18–22" (45–56 cm); up to 4' wingspan

Male: Slender, low-flying hawk. Silver-gray with a large white rump patch and white belly. Long tail with faint narrow bands. Black wing tips. Yellow eyes.

Female: dark-brown back, brown streaking on breast and belly, large white rump patch, thin black tail bands, black wing tips, yellow eyes

Juvenile: similar to female, with an orange breast

Nest: ground; female and male construct; 1 brood per year

Eggs: 4–8; bluish white without markings

Incubation: 31–32 days; female incubates

Fledging: 30–35 days; male and female feed the young

Migration: partial migrator, to southern states, Mexico, and Central America; non-migrator in northern half of Oklahoma

Food: mice, snakes, insects, small birds

Compare: Slimmer than the Red-tailed Hawk (p. 193). Look for a low-gliding hawk with a large white rump patch to identify the male Harrier.

Stan's Notes: One of the easiest of hawks to identify. Glides just above the ground, following the contours of the land while searching for prey. Holds its wings just above horizontal, tilting back and forth in the wind, similar to Turkey Vultures. Formerly called the Marsh Hawk due to its habit of hunting over marshes. Feeds and nests on the ground. Will also preen and rest on the ground. Unlike other hawks, mainly uses its hearing to find prey, followed by sight. At any age, has a distinctive owl-like face disk.

female
p. 181

male

Gadwall
Mareca strepera

Size: 19" (48 cm)

Male: A plump gray duck with a brown head and a distinctive black rump. White belly. Chestnut-tinged wings. Bright-white wing linings. Small white wing patch, seen when swimming. Gray bill.

Female: similar to female Mallard, a mottled brown with a pronounced color change from dark-brown body to light-brown neck and head, bright-white wing linings, small white wing patch, gray bill with orange sides

Juvenile: similar to female

Nest: ground; female lines the nest with fine grass and down feathers plucked from her chest; 1 brood per year

Eggs: 8–11; white without markings

Incubation: 24–27 days; female incubates

Fledging: 48–56 days; young feed themselves

Migration: complete, to Oklahoma, southern states, and Mexico

Food: aquatic plants and insects

Compare: Male Gadwall is one of the few gray ducks. Look for its distinctive black rump.

Stan's Notes: A duck of shallow marshes. Consumes mostly plant material, dunking its head in water to feed rather than tipping forward, like other dabbling ducks. Walks well on land; feeds in fields and woodlands. Frequently in pairs with other duck species. Nests within 300 feet (90 m) of water. Establishes pair bond in winter.

in flight

Canada Goose
Branta canadensis

YEAR-ROUND

Size: 25–43" (64–109 cm); up to 5½' wingspan

Male: Large gray goose with a black neck and head. White chin and cheek strap.

Female: same as male

Juvenile: same as adults

Nest: platform, on the ground; female builds; 1 brood per year

Eggs: 5–10; white without markings

Incubation: 25–30 days; female incubates

Fledging: 42–55 days; male and female teach the young to feed

Migration: non-migrator; moves around to find open water

Food: aquatic plants, insects, seeds

Compare: Large goose that is rarely confused with any other bird.

Stan's Notes: Breeds throughout Oklahoma. Flocks fly in a large V when traveling long distances. Begins breeding in the third year. Adults mate for many years. If threatened, they will hiss as a warning. Males stand as sentinels at the edge of their group and will bob their heads and become aggressive if approached. Adults molt their primary flight feathers while raising their young, rendering family groups temporarily flightless. Several subspecies vary in the U.S. Generally, eastern groups are paler than western. Their size also varies, decreasing northward. The smallest subspecies is in the Arctic.

in flight

Great Blue Heron
Ardea herodias

YEAR-ROUND

Size: 42–48" (107–122 cm); up to 6' wingspan

Male: Tall and gray. Black eyebrows end in long plumes at the back of the head. Long yellow bill. Long feathers at the base of the neck drop down in a kind of necklace. Long legs.

Female: same as male

Juvenile: same as adults, but more brown than gray, with a black crown; lacks plumes

Nest: platform in a colony; male and female build; 1 brood per year

Eggs: 3–5; blue-green without markings

Incubation: 27–28 days; female and male incubate

Fledging: 56–60 days; male and female feed the young

Migration: complete, to southern states, Mexico, and Central and South America; non-migrator in Oklahoma

Food: small fish, frogs, insects, snakes, baby birds

Compare: The Sandhill Crane (p. 255) has a red cap. Look for the long, yellow bill to help identify the Great Blue Heron.

Stan's Notes: One of the most common herons. Found in open water, from small ponds to large lakes. Stalks small fish in shallow water. Will strike at mice, squirrels, and nearly anything it comes across. Red-winged Blackbirds will attack it to stop it from taking their babies out of the nest. In flight, it holds its neck in an S shape and slightly cups its wings, while the legs trail straight out behind. Nests in a colony of up to 100 birds. Nests in trees near or hanging over water. Barks like a dog when startled.

in flight

rusty stain

in-flight
rusty stain

Sandhill Crane
Grus canadensis

Size: 42–48" (107–122 cm); up to 7' wingspan

Male: Elegant gray crane with long legs and neck. Wings and body often rust brown from mud staining. Scarlet-red cap. Yellow to red eyes.

Female: same as male

Juvenile: dull brown with yellow eyes; lacks a red cap

Nest: ground; female and male construct; 1 brood per year

Eggs: 2; olive with brown markings

Incubation: 28–32 days; female and male incubate

Fledging: 65 days; female and male feed the young

Migration: complete, to southern states and Mexico

Food: insects, fruit, worms, plants, amphibians

Compare: Great Blue Heron (p. 253) has a longer bill and holds its neck in an S shape during flight. Look for the scarlet-red cap to help identify the Sandhill Crane.

Stan's Notes: Preens mud into its feathers, staining its plumage rust brown (see insets). Gives a very loud and distinctive rattling call, often heard before the bird is seen. Flight is characteristic, with a faster upstroke, making the wings look like they're flicking in flight. Can fly at heights of over 10,000 feet (3,050 m). Nests on the ground in a large mound of aquatic vegetation. Performs a spectacular mating dance: The birds will face each other, then bow and jump into the air while making loud cackling sounds and flapping their wings. They will also flip sticks and grass into the air during their dance.

male

female

Ruby-throated Hummingbird

Archilochus colubris

SUMMER MIGRATION

Size: 3–3½" (7.5–9 cm)

Male: Tiny, iridescent green bird. Black throat patch reflects bright ruby red in direct sunlight.

Female: same as male but lacks a throat patch

Juvenile: same as female

Nest: cup; female builds; 1–2 broods per year

Eggs: 2; white without markings

Incubation: 12–14 days; female incubates

Fledging: 14–18 days; female feeds the young

Migration: complete, to southern states, Mexico, and Central America

Food: nectar, insects; will come to nectar feeders

Compare: No other bird is as tiny. The Sphinx Moth also hovers at flowers, but it has clear wings, doesn't hum in flight, moves much slower than the Ruby-throated, and can be approached.

Stan's Notes: This is the smallest bird in Oklahoma. Can fly straight up, straight down, or backward and hover in midair. Does not sing but chatters or buzzes to communicate. Weighs about the same as a U.S. penny; it takes about five average-sized hummingbirds to equal the weight of one chickadee. The wings create the humming sound. Flaps 50–60 times or more per second when flying at top speed. Breathes 250 times per minute. Heart beats up to 1,260 times per minute. Builds a stretchy nest with plant material and spiderwebs, gluing pieces of lichen to the exterior for camouflage. Attracted to colorful, tubular flowers. Will extract and eat insects trapped in spiderwebs. A long-distance migrator, wintering as far south as the tropics of Central America.

male

female

Painted Bunting
Passerina ciris

Size: 5½" (14 cm)

Male: An amazing combination of colors. A green back, deep-blue head, and orange chest and belly. Dark wings and tail.

Female: bright green above, light green below

Juvenile: drab version of the female with only some small spots of green

Nest: cup; female and male construct; 1–2 broods per year

Eggs: 3–5; pale blue with brown markings

Incubation: 11–12 days; female incubates

Fledging: 12–14 days; female and male feed the young

Migration: complete, to southern states, the Bahamas, Cuba, Mexico, and Central America

Food: seeds, insects; will visit seed feeders

Compare: No other bird can compare with the male's striking colors. The female is uniquely green and rarely confused with any other bird.

Stan's Notes: A wonderful bunting of backyard gardens, woodland edges, and along brushy roads. Visits seed feeders in wooded yards. Well known for its loud, clear and varied warbling phrases. Cup nest, made of grass and lined with animal hair, is usually in a deep, tangled mass of vines. A common cowbird host, this unfortunately often results in it raising the cowbird young and not its own. Nests across most of Oklahoma. Often captured in Central America and sold as a caged bird; both activities are illegal in the U.S. and should not be supported.

in flight

Green Heron
Butorides virescens

SUMMER

Size: 16–22" (41–56 cm)

Male: Short and stocky. Blue-green back and rust-red neck and breast. Dark-green crest. Short legs are normally yellow but turn bright orange during the breeding season.

Female: same as male

Juvenile: similar to adults, with a bluish-gray back and white-streaked breast and neck

Nest: platform; female and male build; 2 broods per year

Eggs: 2–4; light green without markings

Incubation: 21–25 days; female and male incubate

Fledging: 35–36 days; female and male feed the young

Migration: complete, to South America; some move to Mexico and Central America

Food: small fish, aquatic insects, small amphibians

Compare: Green Heron lacks the long neck of most other herons. Also much smaller than the Great Blue Heron (p. 253). Look for a small heron with a dark green back and crest stalking wetlands.

Stan's Notes: Often gives an explosive, rasping "skyew" call when startled. Holds its head close to its body, which sometimes makes it look like it doesn't have a neck. Waits on the shore or wades stealthily, hunting for small fish, aquatic insects, and small amphibians. Places an object, such as an insect, on the water's surface to attract fish to catch. Nests in a tall tree, often a short distance from the water. The nest can be very high up in the tree. Babies give a loud ticking sound, like the ticktock of a clock.

female
p. 177

male

Wood Duck

Aix sponsa

YEAR-ROUND MIGRATION

Size: 17–20" (43–51 cm)

Male: Small, highly ornamented dabbling duck. Mostly green head and crest patterned with black and white. Rusty chest and a white belly. Red eyes.

Female: brown duck with a bright-white eye-ring, not-so-obvious crest and blue patch on wings (speculum), often hidden

Juvenile: similar to female

Nest: cavity; female lines an old woodpecker cavity or a nest box in a tree; 1 brood per year

Eggs: 10–15; creamy white without markings

Incubation: 28–36 days; female incubates

Fledging: 56–68 days; female teaches the young to feed

Migration: non-migrator in most of Oklahoma

Food: aquatic insects, plants, seeds

Compare: Male Northern Shoveler (p. 267) is larger with a long wide bill. Male Green-winged Teal (p. 171) lacks the Wood Duck's ornamental coloring.

Stan's Notes: A duck of quiet, shallow backwater ponds. Nearly extinct around 1900 due to overhunting, but doing well now. Nests in tree cavity or nest box. Seen flying in forests or perching on high branches. Female takes off with a loud squealing call and enters the nest cavity from full flight. Lays some eggs in a neighboring nest (egg dumping), resulting in more than 20 eggs in some clutches. Hatchlings stay in nest for 24 hours, then jump from as high as 60 feet (18 m) to the ground or water to follow their mother. They never return to the nest.

female
p. 185

male

Mallard

Anas platyrhynchos

YEAR-ROUND

Size:	19–21" (48–53 cm)
Male:	Large, bulbous green head, white necklace, and rust-brown or chestnut chest. Gray-and-white sides. Yellow bill. Orange legs and feet.
Female:	brown with an orange-and-black bill and blue-and-white wing mark (speculum)
Juvenile:	same as female but with a yellow bill
Nest:	ground; female builds; 1 brood per year
Eggs:	7–10; greenish to whitish, unmarked
Incubation:	26–30 days; female incubates
Fledging:	42–52 days; female leads the young to food
Migration:	non-migrator to partial in Oklahoma
Food:	seeds, plants, aquatic insects; will come to ground feeders offering corn
Compare:	Male Northern Shoveler (p. 267) has a white chest with rusty sides and a very large, spoon-shaped bill. Breeding male Northern Pintail (p. 187) has long tail feathers and a brown head. Look for the green head and yellow bill to identify the male Mallard.

Stan's Notes: A familiar dabbling duck of lakes and ponds. Also found in rivers, streams, and some backyards. Tips forward to feed on vegetation on the bottom of shallow water. The name "Mallard" comes from the Latin word *masculus,* meaning "male," referring to the male's habit of taking no part in raising the young. Male and female have white underwings and white tails, but only the male has black central tail feathers that curl upward. Unlike the female, the male doesn't quack. Returns to its birthplace each year.

female
p. 183

male

Northern Shoveler

Anas clypeata

YEAR-ROUND
WINTER

Size: 19–21" (48–53 cm)

Male: Medium-sized duck with an iridescent green head, rust sides, white chest. Extraordinarily large, spoon-shaped bill, almost always held pointed toward the water.

Female: brown and black all over, green wing patch (speculum) and a large spoon-shaped bill

Juvenile: same as female

Nest: ground; female builds; 1 brood per year

Eggs: 9–12; olive without markings

Incubation: 22–25 days; female incubates

Fledging: 30–60 days; female leads the young to food

Migration: complete, to Oklahoma, southern states, Mexico, and Central America

Food: aquatic insects, plants

Compare: Male Mallard (p. 265) is similar, but it lacks the large spoon-shaped bill. The male Wood Duck (p. 263) is smaller and has a crest.

Stan's Notes: One of several species of shovelers. Called "Shoveler" due to the peculiar, shovel-like shape of its bill. Given the common name "Northern" because it is the only species of these ducks in North America. Seen in shallow wetlands, ponds, and small lakes in flocks of 5–10 birds. Flocks fly in tight formation. Swims low in water, pointing its large bill toward the water as if it's too heavy to lift. Usually swims in tight circles while feeding. Feeds mainly by filtering tiny aquatic insects and plants from the surface of the water with its bill. Female gathers plant material and forms it into a nest a short distance from the water.

in flight

female
p. 283

male

Common Merganser
Mergus merganser

WINTER

Size: 26–28" (66–71 cm)

Male: Long, thin, duck-like bird with a green head and black back. White sides, chest, and neck. Long, pointed, orange bill. Often looks black and white in poor light.

Female: Same size and shape as the male, with a rust-red head and ragged "hair." Gray body with a white chest and chin.

Juvenile: same as female

Nest: cavity; female lines an old woodpecker hole or a natural cavity; 1 brood per year

Eggs: 9–11; ivory without markings

Incubation: 28–33 days; female incubates

Fledging: 70–80 days; female feeds the young

Migration: complete migrator; winters in Oklahoma

Food: small fish, aquatic insects, amphibians

Compare: Similar size as male Mallard (p. 265), but male Common Merganser has a black back, bright white sides, and a long pointed bill.

Stan's Notes: Seen on any open water during the winter but more common along large rivers than lakes. A large, shallow-water diver that feeds on fish in 10–15 feet (3–4.5 m) of water. Bill has a fine, serrated-like edge that helps catch slippery fish. Female often lays some eggs in other merganser nests (egg dumping), resulting in up to 15 young in some broods. Male leaves female once she starts incubating. Orphans are accepted by other merganser mothers with young. Fast flight, often low and close to the water, in groups but not in formation.

female
p. 307

male

Baltimore Oriole
Icterus galbula

SUMMER MIGRATION

Size: 7–8" (18–20 cm)

Male: Flaming orange with a black head and back. White-and-orange wing bars. Orange-and-black tail. Gray bill and dark eyes.

Female: pale yellow with orange tones, gray-brown wings, white wing bars, gray bill, dark eyes

Juvenile: same as female

Nest: pendulous; female builds; 1 brood per year

Eggs: 4–5; bluish with brown markings

Incubation: 12–14 days; female incubates

Fledging: 12–14 days; female and male feed the young

Migration: complete, to Mexico, Central America, and South America

Food: insects, fruit, nectar; comes to nectar, orange-half, and grape-jelly feeders

Compare: The male Orchard Oriole (p. 273) is much darker orange. Look for the flaming orange to identify the male Baltimore Oriole.

Stan's Notes: A fantastic songster, often heard before seen. Easily attracted to a feeder that offers sugar water (nectar), orange halves, or grape jelly. Parents bring their young to feeders. Sits at the top of trees, feeding on caterpillars. Female builds a sock-like nest at the outermost branches of tall trees. Prefers parks, yards, and forests and often returns to the same area year after year. Seen during migration and summer. Arrives in spring in March to April, and some of the first to leave in the fall (August). Young males turn orange-and-black at 1½ years of age.

female
p. 309

male

first-year
male

Orchard Oriole
Icterus spurius

Size: 7–8" (18–20 cm)

Male: Dark orange with black head, throat, upper back, wings, and tail. White wing bar. Bill is long and thin. Gray mark on lower bill.

Female: olive-green back, dull-yellow belly and gray wings with 2 indistinct white wing bars

Juvenile: same as female; first-year male looks like the female, with a black bib

Nest: pendulous; female builds; 1 brood per year

Eggs: 3–5; pale blue to white, brown markings

Incubation: 11–12 days; female and male incubate

Fledging: 11–14 days; female and male feed the young

Migration: complete, to central Mexico, Central America, and northern South America

Food: insects, fruit, nectar; comes to nectar, orange-half, and grape-jelly feeders

Compare: Similar to male Baltimore Oriole (p. 271), but it is a brighter orange. Look for the dark-orange plumage and all-black head to identify the Orchard Oriole.

Stan's Notes: Named "Orchard" for its preference for orchards. Also likes open woods. Eats insects until wild fruit starts to ripen. Often nests alone; sometimes nests in small colonies. Parents bring their young to bird feeding stations after they fledge. Many people don't see these birds at their feeders very much during the summer and think they have left, but the birds are still there, hunting for insects to feed to their young. One of the last birds to arrive in spring and one of the first to leave in fall. Spends four to five months in Oklahoma. Often migrates with the more abundant Baltimore Oriole.

male

female
p. 95

yellow
male

House Finch
Haemorhous mexicanus

YEAR-ROUND

Size: 5" (13 cm)

Male: Small finch with a red-to-orange face, throat, chest and rump. Brown cap. Brown marking behind eyes. White belly with brown streaks. Brown wings with white streaks.

Female: brown with a heavily streaked white chest

Juvenile: similar to female

Nest: cup, sometimes in cavities; female builds; 2 broods per year

Eggs: 4–5; pale blue, lightly marked

Incubation: 12–14 days; female incubates

Fledging: 15–19 days; female and male feed the young

Migration: non-migrator to partial migrator; moves around to find food

Food: seeds, fruit, leaf buds; visits seed feeders and feeders that offer grape jelly

Compare: Male Purple Finch (p. 277) is very similar, but male House Finch lacks the red crown. Look for the streaked breast and belly, and brown cap of male House Finch.

Stan's Notes: Can be common at feeders. A social bird, visits feeders in small flocks. Likes to nest in hanging flower baskets. Male sings a loud, cheerful warbling song. Historically, it occurred from the Pacific to the Rockies, with only a few reaching the eastern side. Now found across the U.S. Suffers from a disease that causes the eyes to crust, resulting in blindness and death. Rarely, some males are yellow (see inset) instead of red, probably due to poor diet.

female
p. 113

male

Purple Finch
Haemorhous purpureus

WINTER

Size: 6" (15 cm)

Male: Raspberry-red head, cap, chest, back, and rump. Brownish wings and tail. Large bill.

Female: heavily streaked brown-and-white bird with bold white eyebrows

Juvenile: same as female

Nest: cup; female and male build; 1 brood per year

Eggs: 4–5; greenish blue with brown markings

Incubation: 12–13 days; female incubates

Fledging: 13–14 days; female and male feed the young

Migration: irruptive; moves around in search of food

Food: seeds, insects, fruit; comes to seed feeders

Compare: The male House Finch (p. 275) has a brown cap and a streaked belly. Look for the raspberry cap to help identify the male Purple Finch.

Stan's Notes: Usually only seen in the winter, when Purple Finches leave their northern homes and move around in search of food. Travels in flocks of up to 50 birds. Visits seed feeders along with House Finches, which makes it hard to tell them apart. Feeds mainly on seeds; ash tree seeds are an important source of food. Found in coniferous forests, mixed woods, woodland edges, and suburban backyards. Flies in the typical undulating, up-and-down pattern of finches. Sings a rich, loud song. Gives a distinctive "tic" note only in flight. Male is not purple. The Latin species name *purpureus* means "purple" (or other reddish colors).

female
p. 311

male

Summer Tanager
Piranga rubra

SUMMER

Size: 8" (20 cm)

Male: Bright rosy-red bird with darker red wings.

Female: overall yellow with slightly darker wings

Juvenile: male has patches of red and green over the entire body, female is same as adult female

Nest: cup; female builds; 1–2 broods per year

Eggs: 3–5; pale blue with dark markings

Incubation: 10–12 days; female incubates

Fledging: 12–15 days; female and male feed young

Migration: complete, to Central and South America

Food: insects, fruit

Compare: Similar size as the male Northern Cardinal (p. 281), but the male Cardinal has a black mask, large crest, and red bill.

Stan's Notes: Found in Oklahoma, where woodlands exist, especially in mixed pine and oak forests. Due to clearing of land for agriculture, populations have decreased for over a century, especially most recently. Returning to the state in late April and with young hatching in late May, some pairs have two broods per year. While fruit makes up some of the diet, most of it consists of insects such as bees and wasps. Summer Tanagers, unfortunately seem to be parasitized by Brown-headed Cowbirds.

female
p. 139

male

juvenile

Northern Cardinal
Cardinalis cardinalis

Size: 8–9" (20–23 cm)

Male: Red with a black mask that extends from the face to the throat. Large crest and a large red bill.

Female: buff-brown with a black mask, large reddish bill, and red tinges on the crest and wings

Juvenile: same as female but with a blackish-gray bill

Nest: cup; female builds; 2–3 broods per year

Eggs: 3–4; bluish white with brown markings

Incubation: 12–13 days; female and male incubate

Fledging: 9–10 days; female and male feed the young

Migration: non-migrator

Food: seeds, insects, fruit; comes to seed feeders

Compare: Look for the black mask, large crest, and red bill to identify the male Northern Cardinal.

Stan's Notes: A familiar backyard bird. Seen in a variety of habitats, including parks. Usually likes thick vegetation. One of the few species in which both males and females sing. Can be heard all year. Listen for its "whata-cheer-cheer-cheer" territorial call in spring. Watch for a male feeding a female during courtship. The male also feeds the young of the first brood while the female builds a second nest. Territorial in spring, fighting its own reflection in a window or other reflective surface. Non-territorial in winter, gathering in small flocks of up to 20 birds. *Cardinalis* denotes importance, as represented by the red priestly garments of Catholic cardinals.

in flight

male
p. 269

female

Common Merganser
Mergus merganser

Size: 26–28" (66–71 cm)

Female: Long, thin, duck-like bird with a rust-red head and ragged "hair." Gray body and white chest and chin. Long, pointed orange bill.

Male: same size and shape as the female, but with a green head, a black back and white sides

Juvenile: same as female

Nest: cavity; female lines an old woodpecker hole or a natural cavity; 1 brood per year

Eggs: 9–11; ivory without markings

Incubation: 28–33 days; female incubates

Fledging: 70–80 days; female feeds the young

Migration: complete, to southern states and Mexico; winters in Oklahoma

Food: small fish, aquatic insects, amphibians

Compare: Hard to confuse with other birds. Look for a rust-red head with ragged "hair," a white chin and a long, pointed, orange bill to identify.

Stan's Notes: Seen on any open water during the winter but more common along large rivers than lakes. A large, shallow-water diver that feeds on fish in 10–15 feet (3–4.5 m) of water. Bill has a fine, serrated-like edge that helps catch slippery fish. The female often lays some eggs in other merganser nests (egg dumping), resulting in up to 15 young in some broods. Male leaves the female once she starts incubating. Orphans are accepted by other merganser mothers with young. Fast flight, often low and close to the water. Usually not vocal except for an alarm call that sounds like a muffled quack.

in flight

breeding

juvenile

winter

Ring-billed Gull
Larus delawarensis

YEAR-ROUND

Size: 18–20" (45–51 cm); up to 4' wingspan

Male: White with gray wings, black wing tips spotted with white, and a white tail, seen in flight (inset). Yellow bill with a black ring near the tip. Yellowish legs and feet. In winter, the back of the head and the nape of the neck are speckled brown.

Female: same as male

Juvenile: white with brown speckles and a brown tip of tail; mostly dark bill

Nest: ground; female and male construct; 1 brood per year

Eggs: 2–4; off-white with brown markings

Incubation: 20–21 days; female and male incubate

Fledging: 20–40 days; female and male feed the young

Migration: complete, to southern states and Mexico; small percentage don't migrate in Oklahoma

Food: insects, fish; scavenges for food

Compare: A large white-and-gray gull. Look for a black ring near the tip of a yellow bill, and yellow legs and feet.

Stan's Notes: A common gull of garbage dumps and parking lots. One of the most common gulls in the U.S. Hundreds of these birds often flock together. A three-year gull with different plumages in each of its first three years. Attains the ring on its bill after the first winter and adult plumage in the third year. Defends a small area around the nest, usually only a few feet.

in flight

Cattle Egret
Bubulcus ibis

SUMMER MIGRATION

Size: 18–22" (45–56 cm); up to 3' wingspan

Male: White with orange-buff crest, breast and back. Stocky with a disproportionally large round head. Red-orange bill and legs. Winter plumage is all white with a yellow bill and dark legs.

Female: same as male

Juvenile: similar to winter adult but with a dark bill

Nest: platform; female and male build; 1 brood per year

Eggs: 2–5; light blue-green without markings

Incubation: 22–26 days; female and male incubate

Fledging: 28–30 days; female and male feed the young

Migration: complete migrator, to southern states, Mexico, and Central and South America; moves around to find food

Food: insects, small mammals

Compare: Great Egret (p. 291) is about twice as large and has a much longer neck and a much larger bill.

Stan's Notes: Came to South America from Africa around 1880, reaching Florida in the 1940s, and has spread out across the U.S. in recent years. Started being seen in Oklahoma in the mid-1950s. Often seen singularly in pastures, hunting insects at cow and horse pies by wiggling its neck and head back and forth and from side to side, while holding its body still. Then, it stabs at prey and tosses it to the back of its mouth. Frequently attracted to field fires to hunt newly exposed animals and insects. In some years, it is found as far as northern-tier states and Canada.

in flight

Snowy Egret
Egretta thula

SUMMER
MIGRATION

Size: 22–26" (56–66 cm); up to 3½' wingspan

Male: All-white bird with black bill. Black legs. Bright-yellow feet. Long feather plumes on head, neck, and back during breeding season.

Female: same as male

Juvenile: similar to adult, but backs of legs are yellow

Nest: platform; female and male build; 1 brood per year

Eggs: 3–5; light blue-green without markings

Incubation: 20–24 days; female and male incubate

Fledging: 28–30 days; female and male feed the young

Migration: complete, to Gulf Coast and Mexico

Food: aquatic insects, small fish

Compare: Great Egret (p. 291) is much larger and has a yellow bill and black feet. Juvenile Little Blue Heron (p. 87) is the same size and has a black-tipped gray bill. Look for the black bill and yellow feet of Snowy Egret to help identify.

Stan's Notes: Common in wetlands and often seen with other egrets. Colonies may include up to several hundred nests. Nests are low in shrubs 5–10 feet (1.5–3 m) tall, or constructs a nest on the ground, usually mixed among other egret and heron nests. Chicks hatch days apart (asynchronous), leading to starvation of last to hatch. Will actively "hunt" prey by moving around quickly, stirring up small fish and aquatic insects with its feet. In the breeding state, a yellow patch at the base of bill and the yellow feet turn orange-red. Was hunted to near extinction in the late 1800s for its feathers.

in flight

Great Egret
Ardea alba

SUMMER
MIGRATION

Size: 36–40" (91–102 cm); up to 4½' wingspan

Male: Tall, thin, all-white bird with a long neck and a long, pointed yellow bill. Black, stilt-like legs and black feet.

Female: same as male

Juvenile: same as adults

Nest: platform; male and female construct; 1 brood per year

Eggs: 2–3; light blue without markings

Incubation: 23–26 days; female and male incubate

Fledging: 43–49 days; female and male feed the young

Migration: complete, to southern states, Mexico, and Central America

Food: small fish, aquatic insects, frogs, crayfish

Compare: Snowy Egret (p. 289) is much smaller with yellow feet and a black bill. Cattle Egret (p. 287) is about half the size of the Great Egret and has a much shorter neck and much smaller bill. Great Blue Heron (p. 253) is similar in shape, but it is larger and gray in color.

Stan's Notes: A graceful, stately bird. Slowly stalks shallow ponds, lakes, and wetlands in search of small fish to spear with its long, sharp bill. Holds neck in an S shape during flight. Nests in colonies with as many as 100 birds. Gives a loud, dry croak if disturbed or when squabbling for a nest site at the colony. The name "Egret" comes from the French word *aigrette,* meaning "ornamental tufts of plumes." The plumes grow near the tail during the breeding season. Hunted to near extinction in the 1800s and early 1900s for its beautiful long plumes, which were used to decorate hats for women. Today, the egret is a protected species.

blue morph

juvenile

white
morph

in flight

Snow Goose
Chen caerulescens

WINTER

Size: 25–38" (64–97 cm); up to 4½' wingspan

Male: White morph has black wing tips and varying patches of black and brown. Blue morph has a white head and a gray breast and back. Both morphs have a pink bill and legs.

Female: same as male

Juvenile: overall dull gray with a dark bill

Nest: ground; female builds; 1 brood per year

Eggs: 3–5; white without markings

Incubation: 23–25 days; female incubates

Fledging: 45–49 days; female and male teach the young to feed

Migration: complete, to, southern states, New Mexico, California, and Mexico; winters in Oklahoma

Food: aquatic insects and plants

Compare: The Canada Goose (p. 251) is larger and has a black neck and white chin strap. American White Pelican (p. 297) shares black wing tips, but it has an enormous bill.

Stan's Notes: This bird occurs in light (white) and dark (blue) color morphs. The white morph is more common than the blue. A bird of wide-open fields, wetlands, and lakes of any size. It has a thick, serrated bill, which helps it to grab and pull up plants. Breeds in large colonies on the northern tundra in Canada. Female starts to breed at 2–3 years. Older females produce more eggs and are more successful at reproduction than younger females. Seen by the thousands during migration and in winter. Has a classic goose-like call.

in flight

juvenile

Trumpeter Swan

Cygnus buccinator

WINTER

Size:	58–62" (147–157 cm); up to 6½' wingspan
Male:	A large all-white swan with an all-black bill, legs, and feet.
Female:	same as male
Juvenile:	same size as adult, with gray plumage and a pinkish-gray bill
Nest:	ground; female and male construct; 1 brood per year
Eggs:	4–6; cream-white without markings
Incubation:	33–37 days; female incubates
Fledging:	100–120 days; female and male show the young what to eat
Migration:	complete migrator, to southern states
Food:	aquatic plants, insects
Compare:	Snow Goose (p. 293) is much smaller and has black wing tips.

Stan's Notes: Was once eliminated due to market hunting, but reintroduced with great success in northern states. These birds migrate to Oklahoma for winter. Most breeding programs were started with eggs taken from Trumpeters in Alaska. Often on larger rivers. Also in wetlands, marshes, small lakes, ponds, and farm fields. Mated pairs defend large territories and construct large mound nests at the edge of water. Many flock to open water on the Missouri River in winter. Named for its loud, trumpet-like call, typically given in flight.

breeding

in flight

chick-feeding adult

American White Pelican
Pelecanus erythrorhynchos

MIGRATION WINTER

Size: 60–64" (152–163 cm); up to 9' wingspan

Male: Large white pelican with an enormous bright-yellow-to-orange bill. Yellow legs and feet. Black wing tips and trailing edge of wings. Breeding plumage has a bright-orange bill, legs, and feet. Chick-feeding adult (an adult that is feeding young) has a gray-black crown.

Female: same as male

Juvenile: duller white than adult, with a brownish head and neck

Nest: ground, scraped-out depression rimmed with dirt; female and male build; 1 brood per year

Eggs: 1–3; white without markings

Incubation: 29–36 days; male and female incubate

Fledging: 60–70 days; female and male feed the young

Migration: complete, to Oklahoma, southern states, and Central and South America;

Food: fish

Compare: Snow Goose (p. 293) is much smaller and lacks the Pelican's enormous bill. Look for the Pelican's black wing tips in flight.

Stan's Notes: Frequently seen in large groups on the larger lakes and reservoirs of Oklahoma during migration and summer. Doesn't dive to catch fish, like Brown Pelicans (not shown). Instead, groups swim and dip their bills simultaneously into water to scoop up fish. Groups fly in a large V, often gliding, followed by simultaneous flapping. Large flocks swirl on columns of rising warm air (thermals) on hot days. Breeding adults typically grow a flat, fibrous plate on the upper bill, which drops off after the eggs hatch. Usually silent; gives short grunts at the nesting colony.

male

winter
male

female

American Goldfinch
Spinus tristis

Size: 5" (13 cm)

Male: Canary-yellow finch with a black forehead and tail. Black wings with white wing bars. White rump. No markings on the chest. Winter male is similar to the female.

Female: dull olive-yellow plumage with brown wings; lacks a black forehead

Juvenile: same as female

Nest: cup; female builds; 1 brood per year

Eggs: 4–6; pale blue without markings

Incubation: 10–12 days; female incubates

Fledging: 11–17 days; female and male feed the young

Migration: partial migrator to non-migrator; small flocks of up to 20 birds move around to find food

Food: seeds, insects; will come to seed feeders

Compare: The Pine Siskin (p. 93) has a streaked chest and belly, with yellow wing bars. Female House Finch (p. 95) and female Purple Finch (p. 113) both have heavily streaked chests. Male Yellow Warbler (p. 303) is all yellow with orange streaks on chest.

Stan's Notes: A common year-round backyard resident. Most often found in open fields, scrubby areas, and woodlands. Enjoys Nyjer seed in feeders. Lines its nest with the silky down from wild this-tle. Almost always in small flocks. Twitters while it flies. Flight is roller coaster-like. Often called Wild Canary due to the male's canary-colored plumage. Male sings a pleasant, high-pitched song. Moves only far enough south to find food.

male

female

Common Yellowthroat

Geothlypis trichas

SUMMER

Size: 5" (13 cm)

Male: Olive-brown with a bright-yellow throat and chest, a white belly, and a distinctive black mask outlined in white. Long, thin, pointed black bill.

Female: similar to male but lacks a black mask

Juvenile: same as female

Nest: cup; female builds; 2 broods per year

Eggs: 3–5; white with brown markings

Incubation: 11–12 days; female incubates

Fledging: 10–11 days; female and male feed the young

Migration: complete, to southern states, Mexico, and Central America

Food: insects

Compare: The male American Goldfinch (p. 299) has a black forehead and wings. Male Yellow Warbler (p. 303) has fine orange streaks on chest and lacks the black mask. The Yellow-rumped Warbler (p. 213) only has patches of yellow and lacks the yellow chest of the Yellowthroat.

Stan's Notes: A common warbler of open fields and marshes. Sings a cheerful, well-known "witchity-witchity-witchity-witchity" song from deep within tall grasses. Male sings from prominent perches and while he hunts. He performs a curious courtship display, bouncing in and out of tall grass while singing a mating song. Female builds a nest low to the ground. Young remain dependent on their parents longer than most other warblers. A frequent cowbird host.

male

female

Yellow Warbler
Setophaga petechia

SUMMER
MIGRATION

Size: 5" (13 cm)

Male: Yellow with thin orange streaks on the chest and belly. Long, pointed dark bill.

Female: same as male but lacks orange streaks

Juvenile: similar to female but much duller

Nest: cup; female builds; 1 brood per year

Eggs: 4–5; white with brown markings

Incubation: 11–12 days; female incubates

Fledging: 10–12 days; female and male feed the young

Migration: complete, to southern states, Mexico, and Central and South America

Food: insects

Compare: Yellow-rumped Warbler (p. 213) has only spots of yellow, compared with the orange streaking on chest of male Yellow Warbler. The male American Goldfinch (p. 299) has a black forehead and black wings. Look for the orange streaks on the chest to identify the male Yellow Warbler. The female American Goldfinch (p. 299) has white wing bars.

Stan's Notes: A scattered but widespread breeding warbler in the state, more common in eastern portion of Oklahoma. Seen in gardens and shrubby areas close to water. A prolific insect eater, gleaning caterpillars, and other insects from tree leaves. Male sings a string of notes that sound like "sweet, sweet, sweet, I'm-so-sweet!" Begins to migrate south in August. Returns in April. Males arrive in spring before females to claim territories. Migrates at night in mixed flocks of warblers. Rests and feeds during the day.

Dickcissel
Spiza americana

Size: 6" (15 cm)

Male: A small, thick-billed bird with yellow chest, belly and eyebrows. A distinctive black bib under a white chin. Chestnut wings.

Female: same as male, but lacking the black bib

Juvenile: similar to female, only duller overall

Nest: cup, made of plant stems, grass and leaves; female builds; 1 brood per year

Eggs: 4–6; pale blue without markings

Incubation: 12–13 days; female incubates

Fledging: 9–11 days; female feeds young

Migration: complete, to Mexico, Central America, and South America

Food: insects, seeds

Compare: The Eastern Meadowlark (p. 315) is larger and has a prominent black V-shaped necklace unlike the Dickcissel's black bib.

Stan's Notes: Originally a bird of the prairie, now found in alfalfa fields, abandoned fields, and meadows due to the loss of native prairie habitat. Prefers habitat that is sparsely vegetative. Doesn't do well in thick, dense vegetation. The males arrive at breeding sites a couple weeks before the females and begin to sing from prominent perches. Often seen singing from a fence post because it's the tallest object around. Nest is bulky, only a couple feet above ground, and usually well concealed. Common name comes from an imitation of its song.

male
p. 271

female

Baltimore Oriole
Icterus galbula

Size: 7–8" (18–20 cm)

Female: Pale yellow with orange tones and gray-brown wings with white wing bars. Gray bill. Dark eyes.

Male: flaming orange with a black head and back, white-and-orange wing bars, an orange-and-black tail, a gray bill, and dark eyes

Juvenile: same as female

Nest: pendulous; female builds; 1 brood per year

Eggs: 4–5; bluish with brown markings

Incubation: 12–14 days; female incubates

Fledging: 12–14 days; female and male feed the young

Migration: complete, to Mexico, Central America, and South America

Food: insects, fruit, nectar; comes to nectar, orange-half, and grape-jelly feeders

Compare: The female Orchard Oriole (p. 309) has a dull-yellow belly. Look for the gray-brown wings to identify the female Baltimore Oriole.

Stan's Notes: A fantastic songster, often heard before seen. Easily attracted to bird feeders that offer sugar water (nectar), orange halves, or grape jelly. Parents bring young to feeders. Sits at the top of trees, feeding on caterpillars. Female builds a sock-like nest at the outermost branches of tall trees. Prefers parks, yards, and forests and often returns to the same area year after year. Seen during migration and summer. Arrives in spring from March to April, and some of the first to leave in the fall (August). Young males turn orange-and-black at 1½ years of age.

male
p. 273

female

first-year
male

Orchard Oriole
Icterus spurius

Size: 7–8" (18–20 cm)

Female: Olive-green with a dull-yellow belly. Gray wings with 2 indistinct white wing bars. Long, thin bill with a gray mark on the lower bill.

Male: dark orange with black head, throat, upper back, wings, and tail; 1 white wing bar

Juvenile: same as female; first-year male looks like the female, with a black bib

Nest: pendulous; female builds; 1 brood per year

Eggs: 3–5; pale blue to white, brown markings

Incubation: 11–12 days; female and male incubate

Fledging: 11–14 days; female and male feed the young

Migration: complete, to central Mexico, Central America, and northern South America

Food: insects, fruit, nectar; comes to nectar, orange-half, and grape-jelly feeders

Compare: The female Baltimore Oriole (p. 307) is similar, but it has orange tones and more pronounced wing bars. Female Summer Tanager (p. 311) is mustard yellow with a larger, thicker bill.

Stan's Notes: Named "Orchard" for its preference for orchards. Also likes open woods. Eats insects until wild fruit starts to ripen. One of the last birds to arrive in spring and one of the first to leave in fall. Often nests alone; sometimes nests in small colonies. Parents bring their young to bird feeding stations after they fledge. Many people don't see these birds at feeders much during the summer and think they have left, but the birds are still there, hunting for insects to feed to their young.

male
p. 279

female

Summer Tanager
Piranga rubra

Size: 8" (20 cm)

Female: Some show a faint wash of red, but most females are a mustard-yellow overall with slightly darker wings.

Male: bright rosy-red bird with darker red wings

Juvenile: male has patches of red and green over the entire body, female is same as adult female

Nest: cup; female builds; 1–2 broods per year

Eggs: 3–5; pale blue with dark markings

Incubation: 10–12 days; female incubates

Fledging: 12–15 days; female and male feed young

Migration: complete, to Central and South America

Food: insects, fruit

Compare: Female Orchard Oriole (p. 309) and Baltimore Oriole (p. 307) are similar, but they have wing bars. Look for Summer Tanager's lack of wing bars and larger, thicker bill to identify.

Stan's Notes: Found throughout parts of Oklahoma where woodlands exist, especially in mixed pine and oak forests. Due to clearing of land for agriculture, populations have decreased for over a century, especially most recently. Returning to the state in late April and with young hatching in late May, some pairs have two broods per year. While fruit makes up some of the diet, most of it consists of insects such as bees and wasps. Summer Tanagers unfortunately, seem to be parasitized by Brown-headed Cowbirds.

Western Kingbird
Tyrannus verticalis

SUMMER
MIGRATION

Size: 9" (22.5 cm)

Male: Bright-yellow belly and yellow under wings. Gray head and chest, often with white chin. Wings and tail are dark gray to nearly black with white outer edges on tail.

Female: same as male

Juvenile: similar to adult, less yellow and more gray

Nest: cup; female and male construct; 1 brood per year

Eggs: 3–4; white with brown markings

Incubation: 18–20 days; female incubates

Fledging: 16–18 days; female and male feed young

Migration: complete, to Central America

Food: insects, berries

Compare: The Eastern Kingbird (p. 223) lacks any yellow of the Western Kingbird. Eastern Meadowlark (p. 315) also shares the yellow belly of Western Kingbird, but it has a distinctive black V-shaped necklace.

Stan's Notes: A bird of open country, frequently seen sitting on top of the same shrub or fence post. Hunts by watching for crickets, bees, grasshoppers, and other insects and flying out to catch them, then returns to perch. Parents teach young how to hunt, bringing wounded insects back to the nest for the young to chase. Returns in April. Builds nest in May, often in a fork of a small single-trunk tree. More common in western and central Oklahoma, where it nests in trees around homesteads and farms.

Western
Meadowlark

Eastern Meadowlark
Sturnella magna

Size: 9" (22.5 cm)

Male: Heavy-bodied bird with a short tail. Yellow chest and brown back. Prominent V-shaped black necklace. White outer tail feathers.

Female: same as male

Juvenile: same as adult

Nest: cup, on the ground in dense cover; female builds; 2 broods per year

Eggs: 3–5; white with brown markings

Incubation: 13–15 days; female incubates

Fledging: 11–13 days; female and male feed young

Migration: complete, to southern states, Mexico, and Central America; non-migrator in Oklahoma

Food: insects, seeds

Compare: Western Kingbird (p. 313) shares the yellow belly, but it lacks the V-shaped black necklace. Horned Lark (p. 129) lacks the yellow chest and belly. Look for a black V marking on the chest to help identify the Meadowlark.

Stan's Notes: A bird of open grassy country. Named "Meadowlark" because it's a bird of meadows and sings like the larks of Europe. Best known for its wonderful song—a flute-like, clear whistle. Not in the lark family; a blackbird family member and is related to grackles and orioles. Like other members of the blackbird family, the meadowlark catches prey by poking its long thin bill in places such as holes in the ground or tufts of grass, where insects are hiding. The Western Meadowlark (see inset is nearly identical in appearance, but is less common and sings a different song. Western Meadowlarks can be found in the western half of Oklahoma year-round and in eastern Oklahoma in winter.

BIRDING ON THE INTERNET

Birding online is a great way to discover additional information and learn more about birds. These websites will assist you in your pursuit of birds. Web addresses sometimes change a bit, so if one no longer works, just enter the name of the group into a search engine to track down the new address.

Site	Address
Author Stan Tekiela's homepage	naturesmart.com
American Birding Association	aba.org
The Cornell Lab of Ornithology	birds.cornell.edu
eBird	ebird.org
Oklahoma City Audubon Society	okc-audubon.org
Oklahoma Ornithological Society	okbirds.org
Tulsa Audubon Society	tulsaaudubon.org
WildCare Oklahoma	wildcareoklahoma.org

CHECKLIST/INDEX BY SPECIES

Use the boxes to check the birds you've seen.

ABOUT THE AUTHOR

Naturalist, wildlife photographer, and writer Stan Tekiela is the originator of the popular state-specific field guide series that includes the *Birds of Texas Field Guide*. Stan has authored more than 190 educational books, including field guides, quick guides, nature books, children's books, and more, presenting many species of animals and plants.

With a Bachelor of Science degree in natural history from the University of Minnesota, and as an active professional naturalist for more than 30 years, Stan studies and photographs wildlife throughout the United States and Canada. He has received national and regional awards for his books and photographs and is also a well-known columnist and radio personality. His syndicated column appears in more than 25 newspapers, and his wildlife programs are broadcast on a number of Midwest radio stations. You can follow Stan on Facebook and Twitter or contact him via his website, naturesmart.com.